The Unspeakable Level

Korzybski's Razor and Other
Ways of Revealing

BY CHRISTOPHER MAYER

INSTITUTE OF GENERAL SEMANTICS

Copyright © 2025 by Christopher W. Mayer
All rights reserved. No part of this publication may be reproduced or transmitted in any form or by any means, electronic or mechanical, including photocopying, recording, or by any informationstorage, and retrieval system, without permission in writing from the publisher.

Published by Institute of General Semantics
401 Park Avenue South, Suite 873 New York, New York 10016
www.generalsemantics.org

ISBN: 9781970164381

Front Cover and Interior Book Design by Matthew Scott Mayer
www.matthewscottmayer.carbonmade.com

Library of Congress Cataloging-in-Publication Data

Names: Mayer, Christopher W., 1972- author

Title: The unspeakable level : Korzybski's razor and other ways of revealing / Christopher Mayer.

Description: [New York, NY] : [Institute of General Semantics], [2025] | Series: New non-Aristotelian library | Includes bibliographical references and index. | Summary: "The unspeakable level is Korzybski's term for that swirl of events language cannot fully capture. It is all that 'is.' Our abstractions—names, descriptions, etc.—often hide and obscure this unspeakable level. In this volume, the author looks at various ways to get behind these abstractions. Korzybski's Razor is one such tool, which knocks many lofty sounding terms off their pedestals. Another chapter explores the nature of polarities, drawing on insights from Meister Eckhart, Pseudo-Dionysius, Carl Jung and many others. Subsequent chapters, through the lens of Korzybski's general semantics, explore various ways of revealing; insights from dreams, Indian sages, Hermes Trismegistus, Christian mystics, Gurdjieff, alchemy, tarot and more. This brisk volume boldly pushes you to explore the boundaries of language, reach that unspeakable level and see the world with fresh eyes"–Provided by publisher.

Identifiers: LCCN 2025030194 (print) | LCCN 2025030195 (ebook) | ISBN 9781970164381 trade paperback | ISBN 9781970164398 epub

Subjects: LCSH: General semantics | Korzybski, Alfred, 1879-1950

Classification: LCC B820 .M39 2025 (print) | LCC B820 (ebook)

LC record available at https://lccn.loc.gov/2025030194

LC ebook record available at https://lccn.loc.gov/2025030195

Other Titles in the IGS Book Series
NEW NON-ARISTOTELIAN LIBRARY

Korzybski, Alfred (2010). *Selections from Science and Sanity.* (2ⁿᵈ Ed.). Edited by Lance Strate, with a Foreword by Bruce I. Kodish. Fort Worth, TX: Institute of General Semantics.

Strate, Lance (2011). *On the Binding Biases of Time and Other Essays on General Semantics and Media Ecology.* Fort Worth, TX: Institute of General Semantics.

Anton, Corey (2011). *Communication Uncovered: General Semantics and Media Ecology.* Fort Worth, TX: Institute of General Semantics.

Levinson, Martin H. (2012). *More Sensible Thinking.* New York, NY: Institute of General Semantics.

Anton, Corey & Strate, Lance (2012). *Korzybski and...* (Eds.) New York, NY: Institute of General Semantics.

Levinson, Martin H. (2014). *Continuing Education Teaching Guide to General Semantics.* New York, NY: Institute of General Semantics.

Berger, Eva & Berger, Isaac (2014). *The Communication Panacea: Pediatrics and General Semantics.* New York, NY: Institute of General Semantics.

Pace, Wayne R. (2017). *How to Avoid Making A Damn Fool of Yourself: An Introduction to General Semantics.* New York, NY: Institute of General Semantics.

Lahman, Mary P. (2018). *Awareness and Action: A Travel Companion.* New York, NY: Institute of General Semantics.

Levinson, Martin H. (2018). *Practical Fairy Tales For Everyday Living, Revised Second Edition.* New York, NY: Institute of General Semantics.

Levinson, Martin H. (2020). *Sensible Thinking for Turbulent Times: Revised Second Edition.* New York, NY: Institute of General Semantics.

Other Titles in the IGS Book Series
NEW NON-ARISTOTELIAN LIBRARY

Mayer, Christopher (2021). *How Do You Know?: A Guide to Clear Thinking About Wall Street, Investing, and Life.* New York, NY: Institute of General Semantics.

Levinson, Martin H. (2021). *Practical Fairy Tales For Everyday Living, Revised Second Edition.* New York, NY: Institute of General Semantics. (In Spanish)

Levinson, Martin H. (2021). *Practical Fairy Tales For Everyday Living, Revised Second Edition.* New York, NY: Institute of General Semantics. (In Hebrew)

Mayer, Christopher (2022). *Dear Fellow Time-Binder: Letters on General Semantics.* New York, NY: Institute of General Semantics.

Liñán, Laura Trujillo (2022). *Formal Cause in Marshall McLuhan's Thinking: An Aristotelian Perspective.* New York, NY: Institute of General Semantics.

Strate, Lance (2022). *Concerning Communication: Epic Quests and Lyric Excursions Within the Human Lifeworld.* New York, NY: Institute of General Semantics.

Korzybski, Alfred (2023). *Science and Sanity: An Introduction to Non-Aristotelian Systems and General Semantics* (6th Ed.) New Preface by Lance Strate, New York, NY: Institute of General Semantics.

Korzybski, Alfred (2024). *General Semantics Seminar 1937: Olivet College Lectures.* (4th Ed.) New York, NY: Institute of General Semantics.

Strate, Lance (2024). *Not A, Not Be, &c.* New York, NY: Institute of General Semantics.

Korzybski, Alfred. (2024). *Science et Sanité, une introduction aux systèmes Non-Aristotéliciens et à la sémantique générale.* New York, NY: Institute of General Semantics.

Levinson, Martin H. (2025). *Sensible Thinking 3: The Adventure Continues.* New York, NY: Institute of General Semantics

*"The development of my ideas
has been the industry of 30 years.
I did not know as I ever should get to
publish them, they're ripening seemed so slow.
But the Harvest Time Has come, at last, and
to me that Harvest seems a wild one, but of
course it is not I who have to pass judgment.
It is not quite you, either, individual reader;
it is experience and history."*

C.S. PEIRCE [1839-1914]

***

*"Every transformation demands as its precondition
'the ending of a world'—the collapse
of an old philosophy of self."*

C.G. JUNG [1875-1961]

TABLE OF CONTENTS

Foreword — XI

Preface — XII

CHAPTER ONE
Korzybski's Razor — 1

CHAPTER TWO
Interlude: Dreams — 41

CHAPTER THREE
Polarities — 61

CHAPTER FOUR
Who Is This "I"? — 87

CHAPTER FIVE
Interlude Part 2: The Shadow — 115

CHAPTER SIX
The World 'Out There' — 137

CHAPTER SEVEN
Hermes Trismegistus — 163

CHAPTER EIGHT
Reflections: Beyond Polarities, Beyond Concepts — 179

CHAPTER NINE
Mutus Liber: By Way of a Conclusion and a Way Forward — 203

Bibliography — 225

Index — 231

FOREWORD

What is the "Unspeakable Level"?

BY GEMINI

Author's Note: Google's Chatbot AI Gemini composed the following Foreword in answer to the question "What is the 'unspeakable level' in Alfred Korzybski's work?" (I'll introduce Korzybski and his work later). I've edited Gemini's response for length, but the words are otherwise untouched.

***

Alfred Korzybski's concept of the "unspeakable level" is fundamental to his General Semantics. Here's the breakdown:

• This is the level of direct experience, the actual events and processes of the world. It's the "territory" that our language "maps."

• Korzybski emphasized that this level is fundamentally non-verbal. It's what "is" before we apply any words or labels to it.

• Therefore, it is "unspeakable" because language, by its very nature, is an abstraction of this level.

Key Concepts:

- **"The map is not the territory":** This famous phrase encapsulates the idea that our words and symbols are not the actual reality they represent. The objective level is the "territory," and our language is the "map."
- **Abstracting:** Korzybski highlighted that our nervous systems constantly abstract from reality, selecting and filtering information. Language further abstracts this process.
- **Structural Differential:** This is a visual aid he developed to help people understand the process of abstracting, and to show that words can never fully encompass the objective level.

In Essence:

- The "unspeakable level" is the raw, unprocessed reality that exists before our interpretations and linguistic representations.
- Korzybski stressed the importance of being aware of this level to avoid confusing our abstractions with reality itself.

Therefore, when you encounter the "unspeakable level" within Korzybski's work, understand it to be the base reality that exists outside of human language.

PREFACE

All and Everything

"In the middle of a circle drawn on the ground stood one of the little boys, sobbing and making strange movements, and the others were standing at a certain distance laughing at him. I was puzzled and asked what it was all about.

"I learned that the boy in the middle was a Yezidi, that the circle had been drawn round him and that he could not get out of it until it was rubbed away... I ran up to him and quickly rubbed out part of the circle, and immediately he dashed out and ran away as fast as he could."

—Gurdjieff, *Meetings with Remarkable Men* [P.65]

***

ou may find it is easy to laugh at such a superstition, held by the poor Yezidi boy, but are you and I so different?

I remember driving along a country road not far from my house. The seldom-travelled road cuts through open fields. I reach an intersection and see a stop sign. The landscape is such that I can see a mile in any direction. No one is coming as far as the eye can see. And yet I stopped. I remember thinking, "Why am I stopping? There is no one around for miles." The stop sign caused an unthinking reaction that overrode a certain common sense. Such behavior is no different than the Yezidi boy Gurdjieff observed.

Of course, stopping at a stop sign when there is no one around for miles is a gentle and benign reaction, even if unthinking and unnecessary. There are a host of other similar situations we might think of, some not so benign. When you start to think about various elements of your life, you start to realize a great deal of what happens is not much different than my automatic reaction at that stop sign.

Think about the clothes you are wearing. How did you come to acquire them? Surely you can think of things you own that you would not own if you had not seen or heard a certain advertising pitch. The ad pushed a certain button or planted a certain desire, and the outcome was inevitable.

Or maybe you saw someone else wearing these clothes and decided you wanted them too. You must now have what only moments before you did not know even existed. What sorcery is this? I'm reminded of a line from *The Cloud of Unknowing*: "It is not a will nor a desire but something which you are at a loss to describe, which moves you to desire you know not what."

How did you choose your car? What about the foods you buy? Or anything you buy? What beliefs and assumptions underlie your purchases and where did they come from?

Put all these together, and we are talking about some of the essential building blocks of a human life. But there is more. Think more broadly about your own life.

What about your political views and religious beliefs? Do you have your own Yezidi circles? And these beliefs, were you born into them or did you choose them freely? And what does that even mean, "choose them freely"? Does it matter?

Search deeply enough and you will come to discover how images, words, concepts, and ideas rule our world almost unseen and almost unquestioned. Almost. But behind these lie something else, the unspeakable level.

Stuff Happens

We are not so much the doers as we like to think. A great deal just seems to happen, in the same way snow melts in the sun's rays and rain falls from the clouds and dust blows in the wind (to borrow Gurdjieffian metaphors). It's not as if we all sat down and decided, after much deliberation and thought, that it would be a good idea to have everyone carrying around cell phones in their pockets. It just sort of happened that way.

And likewise, when you sit and think about your life, you must come to see how much of it was not really your doing. As my daughter likes to say, "I didn't ask to be born." There seem to be a lot of "givens." Like how tall you are. Or your first language.

Everything happens. Everything is connected to everything else. And everything is the way it is because everything else is the way it is. (I can't resist adding Carl Sagan's quip: "If you wish to make an apple pie from scratch, you must first invent the universe.") I'm going to let these ideas sit here largely as assertions for now, but I'll expand on them as we go along.

These ideas are important in what follows. I want to break them up into easy-to-remember verses, like a philosopher of antiquity. After all, Parmenides, for all his importance as a philosopher and logician, wrote in verse. Empedocles did too, too.

So here then is my version of these all-important ideas:

> *Everything happens.*
> *Everything is connected*
> *to everything else.*
> *And everything is the way it is*
> *because <u>everything else</u> is*
> *the way <u>it</u> is.*

Accepting "everything happens" makes it harder to complain about the world. Consider the classic old man rant. You've heard it before: Everything is going to hell. Exhibit A, courtesy of Cecil Lewis, from his *A Wish to Be*, published when he was 97:

> Our materialistic money-grubbing has led us swiftly to a bankrupt world, bogged down in poverty and debt, crippled by fanatical wars and feuds, impotent in the face of murder, brutality and corruption, and at the mercy of every form of self-indulgence, laziness and waste...

Ironically, Lewis led an amazing and adventurous life: WWI fighter ace, BBC founding member, author of several books and radio plays, director of the first two films made of Bernard Shaw's plays, Oscar winner, Tahitian beachcomber, WWII pilot, South African sheep farmer, and after all that, he retired on the picturesque Greek island of Corfu.

With such a rich and full life, it's a wonder to me he found so much to dislike and complain about in his late life memoir. But people love to talk about how the world is going to pot, and how much better things used to be!

I resist this urge. In fact, I find it easy to dismiss—because I fully embrace the wisdom of "everything happens." In a sense, there is nothing to criticize. Everything is as it must be; everything happened the way it had to happen. There is nothing out of place.

Lewis writes the world is 'imperfect,' which most people would probably agree. (I use the single quotes here to flag a problematic term; I'll explain below.) But according to the wisdom of "everything happens," notions of 'perfect' or 'imperfect' don't come into the picture. I know this is hard to swallow right now; I'll develop this idea as we go along.

But we are not entirely powerless in the grand drama. We can cultivate an awareness of what is going on. We can tame the magic and even use it to our advantage. We can become the masters of our symbols. We must try. Or else, as Alfred Korzybski long ago noted, who rules our symbols will rule us. (More about Korzybski in a moment.)

To circle back to Gurdjieff's story: Gurdjieff recounts the Yezidi episode from his youth and recalls being deeply puzzled by the boy's behavior. He asks his elders—professional men, educated men—why the Yezidi boy refused to step out of the circle.

Gurdjieff gets all kinds of answers, most are simply ignorant (but no less surely delivered) prejudicial reasons against the Yezidis and their beliefs. He was not satisfied with their answers, as a broader question gnawed at him for days: What is 'true'? Is it what is in books? Is it what is taught by his teachers? Or are the 'facts' he keeps running up against 'true'?

The 'fact' is that the circle in no way physically held the Yezidi boy from stepping outside of it. Yet, as a symbol it was so powerful the boy may well have been stuck at the bottom of a deep well.

I, too, find myself utterly fascinated by the spell-binding powers of such symbols made by human minds, the fetters we put on our thoughts, the blinders we willingly wear.

Meditating on this state of affairs, and what practical steps one might take to ameliorate it, is what inspired me to write this book. And that entails piercing our abstractions and being mindful of the unspeakable level.

Korzybski and Gurdjieff

As part of my preface, I would like to give a short introduction to Alfred Korzybski and also George Gurdjieff, as I intend to freely use the wisdom of these sages in what follows.

Alfred Korzybski (1879-1950) can be a difficult thinker to recommend. His magnum opus *Science and Sanity* brims with acute insights but it is a long and hard-to-read book. Nonetheless, I find his work essential and worth the effort. Korzybski popularized the phrase "the map is not the territory," a phrase that sums up the chief concern of his life's work: what we say a thing is, is not the thing itself. Believing otherwise leads to all kinds of trouble.

To deal with these challenges, he created a system—a set of interlocking tools and ideas—that he called general semantics. I like to think of general semantics as an aid to critical thinking. I hesitate to give a fuller definition at this point. Definitions are such dead things. Instead, I will use the tools and ideas as we go along, and you'll get a better understanding of general semantics that way—in the same way, maybe, that one would more readily recognize the usefulness of a hammer by watching someone else use it to drive nails in a board than by reading a definition of what a hammer 'is.'

My own study of general semantics has been life-changing. I've written two other books on the subject, and I joined the board of trustees of the Institute of General Semantics, which aims to promote and preserve Korzybski's ideas.

Korzybski is a more obscure figure today, but he had his day in the sun. For a time, many flocked to his seminars and lectures. Among these were some rather famous personalities, including William Burroughs, Buckminster Fuller, Robert Heinlein, Abraham Maslow, and others. *Science and Sanity* has been through six editions now and remains in print.

I don't want to give a potted history of the man, with the usual dates and places and he 'was' this and he 'did' that narrative. You can find that in other places readily enough. I just want you to know I owe a great debt to Korzybski—if it isn't obvious enough. And I want you to at least have a general sense of why he's important.

As for George Gurdjieff (d. 1949), he is an even more difficult figure to categorize. He led a colorful life, full of incident and adventure. He pops into history in Moscow c. 1915, after years of searching and wandering, mostly in the near east. He flees the Russian Revolution, which takes him and a small band of followers through the Caucasus. He winds up in France, sets up an institute, attracts all kinds of literary and artistic talents who come to learn from him. More adventures ensue. There are several good biographies on Gurdjieff, though my favorite still remains the one by James Moore.

Though most of his teaching seems to be oral (there are several books of his "talks") and unfold in his way of living, he did leave a magnum opus; a 1,200-page meandering book titled *All and Everything: An Objectively Impartial Criticism of the Life of Man or Beelzebub's Tales to His Grandson*. There is also a library of books written by his students and others who spent time with him—good reading for those who wish to get into Gurdjieff's world.

There is a wonderful weirdness in Gurdjieff's ideas, but do not be too hasty in judging him. Gurdjieff taught an esoteric system of ideas called the Fourth Way, a method for personal development and spiritual liberation. I think of it as a sort of psychology, and Gurdjieff had interesting things to say about people's attention, or lack of it. Gurdjieff thought most people went about their day to day in a kind of waking sleep.

Here again, I don't want to give you a potted history of Gurdjieff's life and ideas. What I give you here is more of a tease. And, as I have with Korzybski, I have also studied Gurdjieff's ideas for years. They have made a positive impact on me and I want to acknowledge my debt to him here as well. Though not as primary as Korzybski in what follows, his influence looms large enough.

Housekeeping Notes on What Follows

I'm not pretending to write a comprehensive treatment of the ideas covered. It's more of a personal reflection and meditation. I intend for the book to be read and enjoyed and reflected on; and whatever wisdom it offers to be applied in your own life. To that end, there are no footnotes and my bibliography is eclectic and personal.

Another point: There is a certain amount of repetition in what follows. I like to repeat words and phrases and ideas. I am reminded of what Peter Kingsley (in *Catafalque*) once wrote about Carl Jung, about Jung's "fondness for repetition: through circling with his words around the same subjects, time and time again." (Jung: "My thinking is circular; I circle around questions repeatedly. That method is congenial to me.")

I can relate, because I like to do that too. You never know what you might find: a certain expression, a certain metaphor or "way in" to a question may give you the idea that finally sticks. And you may never have found it if you allow yourself only one pass. Repetition is a way of learning, a way of having ideas soak in. (Similar to learning music.) I sometimes wonder why I keep reading and re-reading certain books and passages over and over again. But then I know the value of "refreshing," the value of repetition. To the extent you find a certain repetition herein, just go with it; let the magic of ideas do their thing.

I also want to introduce a set of editorial quirks, which I adopt from Korzybski:

- **The single quotation mark**—which I have already used, designates a word that is used advisedly. It indicates a problematic word, one to use with caution. For example, when discussing Lewis's old man rant, I wrote 'imperfect' doesn't come into play when you look at the world through the lens of the wisdom of everything happens. The single quotation mark around 'imperfect' is meant to flag that word as problematic. What does 'imperfect' mean? Or 'perfect'? Do such states exist? Or are they figments of a particular human imagination? Something to think about and pause over.

- **The date**—Sometimes I might date a name or thing. I might write Korzybski1925 which would indicate I am referring to the Korzybski that existed in 1925. The date is a simple device, meant to highlight that things change. Korzybski in 1925 is not the same as Korzybski in 1945. He had different ideas and experiences by that later date. But we often assume a person is what a person is forever unchanged. In politics, this is particularly acute. People will drag out what somebody said from three decades ago and will want to hold the person today accountable for what was said then. Or even in academia, authors will refer to a certain thinker as if he or she thought the same thing their whole lives. Most of the time, there is not much harm in the casual way people speak about such things. But sometimes there is meaningful change. Korzybski's date is a way to bring attention to the change.

- **The index**—Sometimes I might say Yezidis$_x$, to show that all Yezidis are not the same; they do not all share the same beliefs, etc. Even though we casually use such nouns to label groups of people, the index reminds us that Yezidi$_1$ does not equal Yezidi$_2$. The index can apply to anything, not just groups of people. The orange$_1$ you ate this morning is not the same as the orange$_2$ that remains in the bowl. Each orange is different.

- **The Etc.**—No matter what we say about a person or thing or event or whatever, there are always details we leave out. The use of "etc." accentuates this loss of detail. One of my favorite examples is filmmaker Robert Snyder's description of his father-in-law Buckminster Fuller (1895–1983). Snyder described him as:

> A sailor, a machinist, a comprehensive generalist, a doer, a new former, a student of trends, a technical editor, a businessman, an angel, a quarterback, a lecturer, a critic, an experimental seminarist, a random element, a verb, a comprehensive designer,

an inventor, an engineer, an architect,
a cartographer, a philosopher, a poet,
a cosmogonist, a choreographer, a
visionary, a scientist, a valuable unit,
a mathematician, an air pilot, a Navy
lieutenant, an affable genie, a geometer, a
maverick thinker, a gentle revolutionist, a
lovable genius, an anti-academician, doctor
of science, doctor of arts, doctor of design,
doctor of humanities, an amiable lunatic, a
prophet, the custodian of a vital resource.

And yet—there is more one could say about "Bucky." Hence, if I wanted to bring some attention to this fact, I would add an "etc." at the end. Simple.

Korzybski's three tools embody a certain worldview, which I would characterize as the following:

- What words mean can be tricky (which is where the single quotations are helpful).
- We live in a world of process; nothing stays the same (that's why we use dates).
- No two things, people or events are exactly alike (which is why the index is useful).
- We can never say or know all about anything (hence, etc.).

These are staples of a Korzybskian worldview and they permeate everything that follows; they inspire humility, encourage clarity in word and thought, and help make sense of the world around us.

Abstractions–What Are They?

When I talk about abstractions, I include the following:
- Words: Self-explanatory
- Symbols: Numbers, Circles, Crosses, Hearts, etc.
- Signs: Think road signs or those warnings on electronics about getting an electric shock or those red circles with a line through them as in no guns, etc.
- Images: A white dove with an olive branch, Jesus on a cross, a Norman Rockwell painting

All of these communicate something–an idea or emotion. The categories andwhat we call them are not so important.For example, is an "olive branch" a symbol or an image? You can argue for either, depending. The main idea is that these are all abstractions.

I would exclude from abstractions those experiences that directly appeal to the senses, such as the sound of classical music, the taste of a warm cookie, the touch of a soft fabric, or the scent of freshly baked bread.

"Abstraction" is an ugly, too-long, Latinate word, which means "to draw away." Apropos, as we will see, because abstractions do draw you away from your senses and from "what is going on" in the world—and instead put you in your head. But I can find no better word than abstraction to mean what I mean. And it's easier than repeating words, signs, symbols and images. So we are stuck with it.

Last thoughts: In what follows, I'm going to walk you down some unusual paths. I share dreams. I look at mystical texts, alchemy, even tarot. Yet, the book is full of practical wisdom. In any event, I write to you with great sincerity and honesty. I have no agenda other than to share what I have learned and what has helped me on the path. Since I published it through the Institute of General Semantics, I receive no royalties either. This book is truly a labor of love.

I recall the words of Emerson: "Happy is he... who writes for the love of it... and not from the necessity of sale—who always writes to the unknown friend." All proceeds and royalties from the sale of this book go to the Institute of General Semantics. I write because I love these ideas and hope you will too, my unknown friend.

I've ensured the book has wide margins and ample white space. I would encourage you to use this space to highlight ideas that interest you and take notes. Make the book your own. Add layers, questions, thoughts—and I will do the same. Perhaps we will find better ways to say the unsayable.

With that, let's get into what Korzybski's Razor is and why it's central to our project…

Final note on the plates: The illustrations on the cover and at the chapter heads are drawn from a book called *Mutus Liber*, or the Silent Book. We will get to this later. For now, enjoy the images, which are snapshots of a happy transformation, from sleeping man to a heavenly awakening. May this book facilitate such a transformation in you.

CHAPTER ONE

Korzybski's Razor

Korzybski's Razor (akin in spirit to Ockham's Razor) is a tool, inspired by the works of Korzybski, to cut through the thicket of abstractions that can cloud our understanding. What the Razor does is force us to look at the underlying assumptions embedded in any abstraction. It helps orient us more toward that unspeakable level.

I'll make this all clear in what follows.

To begin, let's start with how I forged the razor out of Korzybski's wise words. And then we'll see some examples of it being put to use.

***

Every word, sign, symbol, and image we use comes freighted with assumptions. Sussing out what those assumptions are, and making them plain for all to see, gets to the core of what Korzybski was all about.

We draw those abstractions from the sea of what we perceive around us. The gap between those abstractions and the sea can be enormous. Gaps create the potential for misunderstandings. And there are always gaps.

As if that were not challenging enough, the very abstractions themselves do not always mean the same thing to every person. Human minds knead doughy definitions over time and shape them as they will. This is why I don't like to argue over definitions. It seems pointless, like trying to fix a shadow on the ground.

Meanings shift across space-time, sometimes dramatically so. George Eliot once wrote "the presence of Nature in all her awful loveliness." Awful here meant "worthy of awe." Not quite what it means in common use today. This is a truth so obvious that I am sure you have your own examples.

So: Meanings seem more like conventions, part of a social agreement. Future generations will not abide by our agreements, anymore than we stuck with those made by the people before us.

Ergo, a good beginning would be to see an abstraction as an abstraction and then to try to understand how a person intends to use it.

Korzybski, in a 1924 paper titled "Time-Binding: The General Theory," laid out the challenge of dealing with abstractions in plain language: "I cannot know what YOU abstract, unless YOU tell ME. Otherwise, the meaning of the symbol MUST be given by a DEFINITION."

As an aside, I find it interesting to note that Korzybski thought a bit differently only a few years earlier when he wrote his 1921 book *Manhood of Humanity*. (Korzybski$_{1924}$ did not think the same way as Korzybski$_{1921}$.) There, in the first chapter, he complains how philosophers write endlessly about words such as 'truth' and 'good' and 'bad.' Yet they never get anywhere because there is no universal agreement as to what the words mean. "If only these words could be scientifically defined," he wrote, "philosophy, law, ethics and psychology would cease to be 'private theories' or verbalism and they would advance to the rank and dignity of sciences."

Later he would give up on trying to fix that shadow on the ground and instead put his focus on the structure of language itself and on the assumptions underlying abstractions more generally. The outcome of this shift was his magnum opus, *Science and Sanity*, published in 1933. But we are getting ahead of ourselves.

Back to the 1924 paper. He goes on to write:

> A man who understands the Anthropometer will never take a word for granted; instead he will ask indefinitely "What do you mean?" and this, ultimately, leads to inquiry into facts, correct symbolism and universal agreement.

He's still got that itch for 'universal agreement', but let's put that aside. As for that bizarre word "Anthropometer"–this was a model Korzybski would later call the Structural Differential. Makes more sense now, doesn't it? Well, just hang on a minute. I love this model and I have a large print of the Structural Differential hanging on my wall to remind me of its wise insights. (See the nearby picture.)

Now is probably a good time to take a short detour and talk about this magical alchemical emblem called the structural differential.

Poor Korzybski had no flair for naming things. He would call his great new discipline, which he expounded on at length in *Science and Sanity*, "general semantics." Thus his followers were doomed forevermore to have to explain what *that* meant and why it was not "semantics," besides saddling them with a clunky label—which several have tried to mollify to no avail—and that would be met with bored stares and rolling eyes by people everywhere ever since.

And so we have "Structural Differential," which is actually a wonderful mnemonic device. I guess it's better than "Anthropometer," but not by much. I would prefer a poetic description, such as "Tree of Perception." Or "Waterfall of Abstracting" to capture the movement implicit in the model, which you will see in a minute.

Korzybski's Structural Differential

The Structural Differential (SD) is worth spending some time on. I use it all the time. As I said, I have a big image of it hanging on my wall in my study at home. At the top is the sea of potential perceptions—the unspeakable level. It's everything that is going on out there, whether you are aware of it or not. That jagged edge at the top indicates this sea extends indefinitely beyond the borders of the model.

From this sea, we take in perceptions. That is the first circle under the sea. The fact

THE UNSPEAKABLE LEVEL

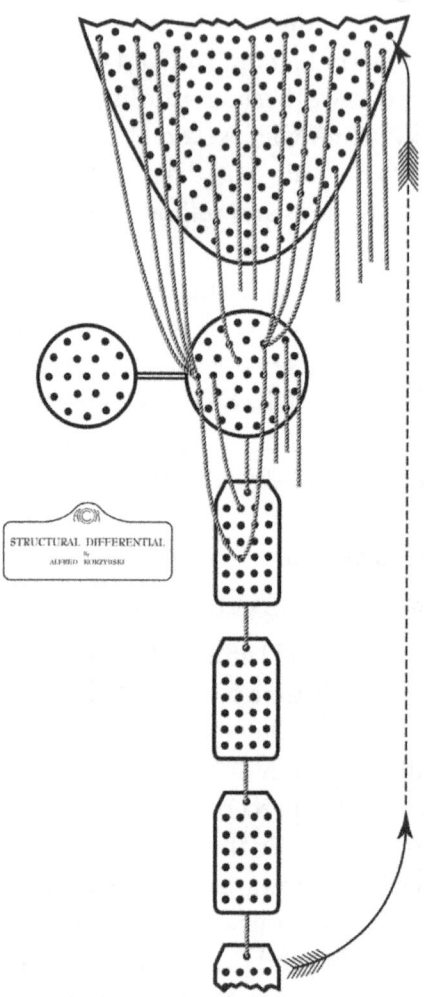

The Structural Differential

that it is smaller and has fewer holes and strings shows our perceptions leave things out. We can't capture or perceive everything. So our perceptions already are partial and incomplete, as they must be. We are still at the nonverbal level here.

From this circle, the flow continues down to another object, which looks like a tag. This is to represent a shift in perceptions, because at this tag we start to transform those perceptions into words. Note again how the tag loses details from the pool of perceptions—there are fewer holes and fewer circles. We are getting further and further away from that rich, deep sea of perceptions from which we began.

As we move down the SD, the next tag loses a few more details and is yet further away from the sea of potential perceptions at top. At these levels, we start to draw inferences and make theories and tell stories. And we build more inferences and theories and stories on top of these. And so and so on; that jagged edge at the bottom of the last tag indicates this is a process that can go on indefinitely, limited only by our imagination and time. It's turtles all the way down.

The arrow that feeds back into the top is meant to show that our ideas color how we perceive what is going on. And it highlights how the process of abstracting is ongoing, constantly drawing from that pool of potential perceptions and going through the whole process all over again. (The separate circle to the left represents other animals, which do not participate in this process. For Korzybski, the distinguishing feature of humanity was our ability to create abstractions and pass them on across generations, a process he called "time-binding.")

This Korzybskian filtering of perceptions is a great reminder that the words we use can be far from the pool of potential receptions from which they began. If I say, "My neighbor Bill's dog," that is pretty close to the top of the funnel. My wife would know exactly what I was referring to. Or if I said "my car," or "my left hand." These are all still abstractions, but they are not far down the chain. In Korzybskian terms, they are "lower order abstractions" in the sense they are close to what is going on out there. Think of "lower order abstraction" as meaning closer to the ground level of experience.

But consider a word such as 'democracy' or 'equality' or 'justice.' These could mean a lot of different things. They are far removed from the top of Korzybski's model. These are examples of a "higher order abstraction." Most everybody writing for magazines and websites, yakking on TV and making political speeches are thoroughly lost in a sea of higher order abstractions. (And that is why it is so easy for them to talk nonsense.)

We ought to value the lower order abstractions more highly than higher order abstractions. Trust life lived close to the ground, closer to what you see, feel, hear, smell, taste, touch. The sand between your toes, the sun in your eyes, the sour taste of lemon on your lips, the heat of a freshly brewed cup of coffee. These are more trustworthy abstractions than when a politician promises 'better education for our children,' or economists tell us 'the economy is strong,' or when a market prognosticator tells us 'stocks are going down.' I would argue these latter phrases don't mean anything at all; they are just gibberish. Noises. For me, they go in one ear and out the other, as the old saying goes.

Thomas Reid (1710–1796) would agree with me insofar as trusting what he could see, feel, hear, smell, touch, and taste over the abstractions of sophists. He wrote one of the greatest passages in all of philosophy in his book *An Inquiry into the Human Mind on the Principles of Common Sense*:

> Let scholastic sophisters entangle themselves in their own cobwebs; I am resolved to take my own existence, and the existence of other things, upon trust; and to believe that snow is cold, and honey sweet, whatever they may say to the contrary. He must either be a fool, or want to make a fool of me, that would reason me out of my reason and senses.

Korzybski talks about a way of ranking or valuing our abstractions, which goes something like this:

- Our perceptions are more important than →
- Non-verbal abstractions drawn from those perceptions, which are more important than →
- Verbal descriptions, which are more important than →
- Inferences drawn from those verbal descriptions, which are more reliable than →
- Inferences drawn from those inferences, and so on down we go... (As I mentioned, it's turtles all the way down!)

The further we get away from the sea of potential receptions, the less reliable our evaluations. Korzybski contended that most of us invert the order here and thus give undue weight to higher order abstractions. Do you feel this is true?

I would say it is. People have all kinds of crazy ideas about the world they got from some talking head somewhere or on the internet or from some book. I am also thinking of the extreme emotions surrounding political candidates, or bubbling over after sporting events. But if people took a moment to look out their window, to be present to what is in front of them, they might behave and think otherwise.

A Digression on 'The News'

I'm reminded of Bill Hicks' bit from *Relentless* (1991). "You know my problem?" the comic says. "I watch too much news... If you ever watch CNN headline news for any length of time it's the most depressing fucking thing you will ever do; 'War, famine, death, AIDS, homeless, recession, depression, war, famine death, AIDS...' Then you look out your window, it's just: [imitates the sound of crickets chirping] Where is all this shit happening man?"

What would Bill Hicks say today with social media running the news cycle 24/7? Every conspiracy theory or every political disagreement seems amplified over these mediums. I often think people would be a lot better off if they never heard or read 'the news.'

'News,' after all, is a product produced by humans. There is no such thing as 'news' out there in the world. What happens on any given day becomes 'newsworthy' because a person or group of people decide it is. And why they choose to highlight one thing over another reflects many factors. Such as, what will make the best headline to get people to watch, listen, click, read, etc. and help sell advertising or subscriptions?

Even when the person or people deciding are trying to be as objective as possible, they still bring with them a host of personal biases, opinions, experiences, etc., which influence their decisions. What a person thinks might be important is contingent on everything else about that person.

You may argue that sometimes, or even often, what's 'news' is obvious. And these obvious subjects would include wars, judicial decisions, presidential announcements, and the like. Even so, someone has to make the judgment call.

The president of the US says lots of things on lots of different days. Wars are ongoing, all over. And so on. Even these apparently obvious newsworthy events involve judgment. Is it the lead story or something else? There are often competing 'events.' There is a war, there is a presidential address, there is a Super Bowl, and there is the death of a celebrity. What gets the spotlight that day? The point is human judgment is always involved.

You may still not be convinced. Surely, you say, there are big events that are obviously important. But if you say this, I will insist the event itself is not news, but people make it so.

As a retort to the idea that there are 'big events' that are so 'obviously news,' I can do no better than to quote Neil Postman, who has certainly been a big influence on my thinking on this matter:

> Of course, some events—the assassination of a president, an earthquake, etc,—have near-universal interest and consequences. But most news does not inhere in the event. An event *becomes* news. And it becomes news because it is selected for notice out

of the buzzing, booming confusion around us. This may seem a fairly obvious point, but keep in mind that many people believe the news is always 'out there' waiting to be gathered or collected. In fact, the news is often *made* than gathered.

(This quote comes from a book titled *How to Watch TV News* by Postman with Steve Powers. Don't be put off by the quaint title. The observations in this book are universal and timeless.)

I think Postman's response is nearly perfect, except for the word "most" as in "most news does not inhere in the event." I would go further. There is no news that inheres in the event. Ever. Even events that seem momentous—such as 9/11 or COVID—were surely matters of indifference to someone, somewhere on this planet. Human beings make these meaningful.

In his book *Amusing Ourselves to Death*, Postman flat out says "the news of the day is a figment of our technological imagination." There was no news of the day back when there was no internet, television or radio. You need these space and distance conquering technologies to create 'news.' "Without a medium to create its form," Postman writes, "the news of the day does not exist." One of the valuable insights I get from Postman's work (and from his teacher, Marshall McLuhan) is this focus on the medium itself as an important feature of the message—as influencing what can be said at all. Or as McLuhan said, "the medium is the message."

And I say the above as someone who was once a prodigious consumer of the news. There was a time when I used to have the *Wall Street Journal*, the *Financial Times*, and the *Washington Post* delivered to my door every day. And I had a digital subscription to the *New York Times*. I also got *Barron's* and *The Economist*. This was earlier in my career as a financial analyst. I didn't want to miss out on anything. I wanted to be 'up to date' and 'informed.'

But I learned that nothing of any lasting importance happens on any given day. Most of the time, the high topic of the week or month or even year is forgotten the following year, or even sooner. The 'news' just doesn't matter.

Life imitates finance in this case. People who sell us the news want us to believe otherwise. But the truth is you can get by quite well without their product. The question of what you allow to absorb your attention is something we will address thoroughly later.

I should also point out that 'news' is, above all, a word. That's it. A concept. An idea. There is no meaning to any word except what people give it. This point is essential to the worldview espoused in this book, and we will come back to it often. You will be amazed at how you can untangle so many human problems with Korzybski's Razor—which I will define anon.

Finally: In this digression on the news, I gave you a glimpse of the Razor in action. But to leave the Structural Differential for the moment: Keep in mind that it, too, is just a model, a way of seeing—or better, a way of revealing. In the end, it, too, is invented.

Back to 1924: "What Do You Mean?"

Let's jump back again to that '24 paper, which Korzybski presented before the International Mathematical Congress in Toronto in August, 1924. Korzybski said one who understood the structural differential would never take a word for granted but would ask "What do you mean?"

Now that you know the structural differential, you can see more where he is coming from. And you can make sense of the quote I shared before: "I cannot know what YOU abstract, unless YOU tell ME. Otherwise, the meaning of the symbol MUST be given by a DEFINITION."

I'm tempted to make that the definitive statement of what I started to think of as Korzybski's Razor. But it doesn't quite capture *exactly* what I wanted to bring out in Korzybski's work. I want to emphasize this idea that human beings make these words, symbols, signs, etc.—and that they don't exist 'out there' in the unspeakable level. Knowing this has a way of disarming those abstractions. But there's even more to it than that.

As I read and re-read Korzybski, I kept seeing flashes of the razor, though never quite a sharp articulation of it, not a pithy hard-punching line I could carve in stone or put on a t-shirt. I kept looking.

I went back to the Olivet Lectures, where Korzybski seemed to be at his most casual and conversational. I reread the famous example of him talking about maps.

In this example, Korzybski talks about a map where San Francisco is shown between Chicago and New York. We know San Francisco is on the west coast, not between Chicago and New York.

What could we say about such a map? We could say it's bad or wrong or false.

Korzybski doesn't like that. "We use moral terms, 'bad' 'wrong' 'false' etc, and nothing of importance follows," he says, "Do we get any wisdom out of such statements? No. That is the point."

For any description, argument, etc., we should focus on the key terms and ask "do we get any wisdom out of it?" And to answer that, you get into key terms and how they are being used. Maybe I found my razor. (Maps, by the way, are fascinating. There are different ways to think about maps beyond what you actually see. A map is also a mapmaker's opinion on what it is safe to ignore. A map shows you the mapmaker's blind spots. Making a map is an effort of deciding what you think is okay to leave out. What maps leave out could be more important than what they leave in. For every map there is an invisible map that shows you what the mapmaker didn't include.)

Earlier in the lecture, Korzybski put the same idea this way: "Every term you use, see how much of evaluation there is in it." Evaluation is a technical term in his scheme. Anytime you like or dislike something, you're evaluating. Any kind of opinion or analysis is an evaluation. It includes reactions, even knee-jerk reactions, and 'emotions,' too, not just 'thinking'. A bit later, Korzybski gives similar advice: "I advise you to work hard on the translation of everyday English terms into human evaluation."

Basically, he's reminding us again that our abstractions don't exist free from human evaluation. Don't assume a dictionary definition.

After reading these various expressions of an idea I found hard to put my finger on exactly, I thought: Maybe I should just state Korzybski's Razor in my own way, in the spirit of Ockham's Razor, who never said exactly what is attributed to him. So I tapped out an idea: Don't accept terms in a description or argument without asking what they mean and why they matter. Recognize these are made by humans and don't exist 'out there.'

Or even more succinctly: *Remember that abstractions are invented by humans. They do not exist independently of humans.*

Or perhaps even better, think of the razor as the second stanza of Korzybski's more popular aphorism:

> The map is not the territory.
> And people make the map.

That's it. That's what I am going to call Korzybski's Razor. The ensuing insights are far-reaching and more profound than they initially appear. Korzybski's Razor helps prevent us from doing what Gurdjieff called "the-pouring-of-the-empty-into-the-void." Idle chatter and nonsense talk. It helps us use our attention wisely.

Words can have an unearned respect and power. The razor denudes them both. Let me show you the razor in action so you'll understand it more clearly and see how liberating it is and how you can use it to answer all kinds of questions.

Buckminster Fuller Using the Razor

Buckminster Fuller (1895–1983) was… well, labels don't suffice. I'm not going to give a potted history of Bucky either, but just talk briefly about what he means to me. Bucky, as he preferred to be called, made ideas sing. He had a beautiful view of the universe as an interlocking system of parts. He was consumed with trying to work with the power of that system and harmonize living human beings with the grand forces of nature. He invented a new type of car with three wheels for greater maneuverability, and he designed a new style of environmentally efficient house that made its own power. He was constantly playing with nature's shapes to do more with less. None of these were commercial successes and all were flawed, but he kept tinkering.

He was a great fan and popularizer of the geodesic dome, which allowed humans to enclose more space with less material and had incredible strength as a structure. Bucky was a great experimenter and talker. He could hold forth for hours, holding audiences spellbound. His ideas were sometimes brilliant and sometimes totally wacky. "Dare to be naive" is one of my favorite sayings of his. He was a modern renaissance man, sketching ideas for bettering the lives of humans in many different disciplines.

Bucky was a bold thinker who epitomizes doing, experimenting, following intuitions, and making stuff with his hands. He was a great builder of models and also somebody who didn't easily fall for abstractions, but was always testing and pushing against what words meant. And not surprisingly, perhaps, he was familiar with Korzybski's work.

Let's see Bucky using the Razor here in an interview by Answar Dil, published in Dil's book *Humans in Universe*, when asked about Einstein (whom he deeply admired):

> Dil: [Banesh] Hoffman, who was Einstein's assistant in 1937... noted "[Einstein] was at heart an artist, employing the medium of science to do his thinking." You wouldn't say that would you?
>
> Fuller: I don't say that.
>
> Dil: What would you say?
>
> Fuller: I would say the word "scientist," the word "artist," and the word "poet," are invented by humans.

That's the Razor. A simple maneuver to call out that the words being used are made by humans. Korzybski's Razor lays open a challenge to the very premise of the question entirely. Bucky's response implies a motherlode of ideas which we will explore in this book. These include:

- Labels are simply words. They are made up, *invented* by humans. What does artist mean? It can mean many things. This very simple reminder dissolves a lot of 'important' questions, as we will see.
- A label, or word, is not the thing or person it tries to describe. Whatever we say about Einstein, those words are not Einstein, the once living person.

- Questions may have no practical importance. What difference does it make if you say Einstein is an 'artist'? Something to consider before you put too much energy into a question.
- Questions may imply either/or answers, but reality is different. In Dil's formulation of the question, Einstein is either an artist or he isn't, which may deny better, more nuanced, answers.
- All such labels or ideas imply polarities. The word artist implies not-artist, but are their gradations in between? An essential aspect of polarities to remember is that they not only imply opposites, but they make opposites necessary. Not life or death, but life *and* death, as Alan Watts once put it; you cannot have one without the other.

But Bucky didn't just use the razor once...

Second Example of Bucky Using the Razor

Bucky used the Razor again in an interview with Martin Pawley, which Pawley included in his 1990 book on Bucky. Pawley calls Bucky a failure because his inventions did not become commercially successful. Bucky replied: "Failure is a word invented by men, there is no such thing as a failure in nature."

It's more powerful than just asking "What do you mean by 'failure'?" Because the counter thrust to this question is not about a definition. It's about questioning the concept of failure itself. Let us riff on some of the various thoughts the Razor could inspire about 'failure.'

We can readily grasp that words may or may not refer to actual things we can point to, see or touch. Thus, there are levels of abstractions. There is no failure in nature; what does failure refer to? We can't point to it. The level of abstraction is high. Remember Korzybski's Structural Differential.

Failure is an *idea*; its opposite is success. The idea of failure cannot exist without success, and vice versa. They are necessary polarities, like up and down. Thinking about failure necessarily means also considering what you think about success.

But there are many gradations in between. And what seems a failure today may be deemed a success tomorrow, or it may seem a necessary stepping stone to a future success. Bucky's inability, for whatever reasons, to develop a commercially successful car allowed him to move on to other projects, projects that perhaps had a greater impact and led to further discoveries he would not have encountered if he had stuck with cars.

Failure, then, sets events in motion. Success, too, sets things in motion. Both failure and success reverberate over time. They are part of a chain of events, a chain for which we cannot discern any real beginning or be sure of any causation. They simply happen. If we pursue the question of causation long enough and deeply enough, we see the world as flux. Everything that happens simply happens.

You can now look at the question of failure in a whole different light. To me, it seems less serious, if not ridiculous, to call some life experiment a failure. As Korzybski put it, "A great many of our human troubles are only artificial verbal bubbles, and when they are pricked they burst so there is nothing left but to laugh." I laugh at those who call any of Bucky's experiments failures. I laugh at the idea of failure. I laugh at success, too. Artificial verbal bubbles are all they are.

Of course, it doesn't mean you just use the Razor all the time and make a nuisance of yourself, pointing out how every word is just a word made up by humans. But used with discretion, the Razor can be a very good tool.

Ramana Maharshi Using the Razor

*"Soul, mind, ego are mere words.
There are no true entities of the kind.
Consciousness is the only truth."*
—Bhagavan

Ever since I gave it a name, Korzybski's Razor, I began to see this same trick used elsewhere. Here is another example from another part of the world and another time.

Imagine the scene: We are at the foothills of Mount Arunachala, at the ashram of the great Indian sage Ramana Maharshi (1879-1950), in southern India. Bhagavan, as he was often called by his devotees, shines as one of the gentlest souls I have ever come across in history.

He was one of the great wisdom teachers of our age, or any age. He seemed to radiate an inner tranquility and often sat in silence. David Godman, who had edited books on Bhagavan and who has devoted most of his life to Bhagavan's teachings, writes in *Be As You Are*:

> Throughout his life Sri Ramana insisted that this silent flow of power represented his teachings in their most direct and concentrated form. The importance he attached to this is indicated by his frequent statements to the effect that his verbal

teachings were only given out to those who were unable to understand his silence.

His fame grew over the years, and in his later life he attracted thousands to sit at his feet. Unlike the sages of antiquity, Bhagavan lived during a time of motor cars and radios and mechanized warfare. We have pictures of a real person, in a real place, living peacefully amidst our busy world.

He had few personal possessions: a water pot, a walking stick, and a loin cloth. He seemed to care for nothing of the usual things that drive human beings; he was unmoved by wealth or fame or sex. He seemed to lack envy entirely; he had no sense of vanity. He refused to be treated as anyone special. Those who brought him gifts, say of special delicacies, would soon find him dividing them among all those who were there. Visitors of all kinds—be they dignitaries or poor peasants—would be treated equally by Bhagavan. He lived his philosophy. He was its greatest exemplar.

It is hard to believe that a man like this actually existed. But we have many written testimonies over many years written by all kinds of people from all over the world. If you do decide to read about him, you will be hard pressed to find anyone saying anything negative about him. There are no scandals. No Rolls Royces. No affairs with students. No fat bank accounts in the Cayman Islands. He was exactly as he appeared to be: A simple human being who had mastered being human.

To me, Bhagavan represents one of the best examples of someone who has seen through all of life's illusions—and who has come as close as one can to that unspeakable level. He was completely at ease with himself, utterly at peace with existence as it was. He showed such a life was possible.

But let us get back to the ashram, at the foothills of Mount Arunachala. It is February 8, 1938. As we read in *Talks with Sri Ramana Maharshi*, three ladies visit the ashram that day; one asks: "What is the best way to work for world peace?"

Bhagavan answers, "What is 'world'? What is 'peace', and who is the 'worker'?"

There it is. The Razor, though, importantly, Bhagavan doesn't point out explicitly—at this point—that such words are invented and do not exist in the world out there. Nonetheless, notice how Bhagavan brings the questioner to a different place. The question is not simply asking for definitions. It's almost rhetorical, bringing a person down the abstraction ladder, closer to the world of experiences. Think again of Korzybski's advice of weighing lower level abstractions more heavily than the higher level.

Bhagavan now brings in explicitly what he had left implied in his initial answer: "The fact is this: the world is only an idea."

And then he has a question of his own: "What do you say: Are you in the world or is the world within you?"

A lady answers: "I am in the world. I am part of it."

"That is the mistake," the sage replies. "The world is only *an idea*."

Here Bhagavan opens a door for discussion. He lets in, a little bit, what the Razor demands you consider. For when you become accustomed to using the Razor, the best answer to Bhagavan's question is obvious and simple: "The world is only an idea."

To say the world is an idea is to set the conversation on firmer ground. Instead of launching into some thought about whether we are in the world or or whether it is within us, it is to say, "Let us question this concept of 'world' first. What do we mean? Is it important? Is it real? What wisdom do we gain from using it?"

Sometimes, the Razor makes it clear to us: There is really nothing more to say, because the concept itself is hollow and pointless, or just ridiculous. Bhagavan makes plain in his response—by using that single word "only"—what he thinks. There is no point in the concept of the world at all, and he is inviting the questioner to drop this line of questioning entirely. Bhagavan discourages 'airy fairy speculation.' Instead he encourages people to come back to themselves, to where they are now, to what they can do now.

The Razor is not meant, necessarily, to be a conversation stopper, although it can function as one, which is perhaps a beneficial feature since so much of the "talk" we are surrounded with is nonsense anyway.

Other Examples of the Razor in Action

Shortly after I wrote the above, I happened to read Anna Challenger's book titled *Philosophy and Art in Gurdjieff's Beelzebub: A Modern Sufi Odyssey*. Challenger convincingly shows how many of Gurdjieff's ideas originate in the teachings of the Sufis.

However, in reading the text, my Korzybski's Razor got a lot of work. I extract one passage in particular:

An obvious question is: "Is Beelzebub's *Tales*, then, art?"; and concurrently, "Is Gurdjieff, then, in the final analysis, an artist?" Many respectable critics, writers, and artists respond with the resounding "Yes." Others could be cited who deny the status of artist to Gurdjieff.

Here again is the obsession over what we call things. The ensuing discussion is not interesting and not enlightening in any way at all. As with the Einstein example earlier, we can ask: What does it matter whether Gurdjieff 'is' an 'artist' or not? 'Artist' is just an idea. It doesn't really mean anything in a practical way. No one ought to read Gurdjieff differently because "many respectable critics" say he is an 'artist.'

A great part of Gurdjieff's teachings aim toward making one less susceptible, even immune, from such outside influences. A basic aspect of Gurjieff's teachings is how much is out of our control, due not only to our own 'hardwiring' but also to untamable cosmic forces. "Still," Challenger writes on page 105, "in spite of cosmic influences, if we were human in the true [read: Gurdjieffian] sense of the word, we would have the inner strength to resist even these powerful outside forces.

In our present state, however, we are at the mercy of all outside impressions."

I am not immune to labels myself, of course. To see through abstractions all the time seems an aspiration. Perhaps it is possible, perhaps not. (Bhagavan, and others we will get to later, show it is possible.) In any event, I aim to try and see. Even then, some abstractions I may willingly allow myself to indulge in for reasons of simple pleasure or convenience. Life is too short to be dogmatic about anything. Even general semantics.

I particularly love the appeal in Challenger's book to "respectable critics." For my part, I say the opinion of such 'respectable critics' on a topic of such pointlessness as "Is Gurdjieff an artist?" is not worth anything. In any event, Korzybski's Razor can cut the influence of such appeals by making plain the absurd nature of the topic at hand.

My criticism of Challenger's text on this point does not mean I didn't enjoy reading the book (I really did) or that I didn't get anything useful out of it (I definitely did). But it means, as with many writers (academics seem particularly prone to this), Challenger used and dealt with many higher order abstractions in a rather carefree way.

Using the Razor allowed a much more critical reading of the text, which enabled me to hone in on essential aspects of Challenger's arguments, ignore the superfluous, and not get lost into the abstractions. People waste a lot of energy arguing for or against names, whereas I seek to neuter the power of naming, period. For me, I'm always bringing things back closer to ground level, to a practical level, cutting away the unnecessary abstractions. This process, you will find, allows you to engage on a deeper level with ideas. You'll read in a different way and learn new things as a result.

I think the Razor reveals something else, too: It exposes our sense of self-importance.

What is the purpose of it all, anyway? What is the meaning of human existence? The ideas of 'purpose' and 'meaning' are human ideas, too. The Universe itself is beyond such concepts and beyond such dualities as 'meaning' and 'meaningless.' Furthermore, there are questions we do not have to work out. We do not have to answer them in the way they are framed.

We will get to these ideas later. For now, it is enough to have presented the basic Razor to you. It is not something to bottle up in a jar of barbicide and put on a shelf. It is a workaday razor, for everyone and anyone, best used frequently. It sharpens with daily use, no stropping required. If you use Korzybski's Razor it will radically alter your view of the world.

Just how, I aim to show in the following chapters...

Another Cut of the Razor: What the Dictionary Says

A footnote to the above discussion: I am always struck when I find an example of someone using the Razor, especially contemporaries. In a *Wall Street Journal* article, Anne Curzan wielded it with skill to take apart an old argument about which words are 'acceptable'.

Take a word such as "irregardless," which is a hideous construction, unnecessarily burdened with an extra and meaningless syllable. I would never use it. But that doesn't mean it's not a 'real word' or is somehow not legitimate. Here is Curzan:

> When people say that a word like "irregardless" isn't a "real" word, I think they mean that it hasn't been legitimized by dictionaries. But who writes dictionaries?

How does a word get included? How different are different dictionaries? I wish more people asked these questions. As a teacher, I am struck that we teach students to question pretty much every text they read, except dictionaries. Here's the thing: **All dictionaries are made by humans**, and they are not timeless. [Bold added.]

Simple isn't it? People make dictionaries. What people? Do they always agree? (No.) Why do they have the authority to say what's what? Historically, the language changes anyway. People use what words they want to use—long before they are blessed by any dictionary. Keeping in mind Korzybski's Razor changes your view on how to think about dictionaries. I'm not saying we throw out dictionaries or that they have no use. What I am saying is that people make dictionaries and that idea brings with it lots of questions.

One more example before we leave this chapter.

The Quest for the Simple Life

The Quest of the Simple Life is a book by William J. Dawson, published in 1906, in which the author moves to the country in

THE UNSPEAKABLE LEVEL

search of a better life—simpler, quieter and less crowded. An old friend criticizes him for it, saying Dawson's move was selfish and he could better help 'society' by being in London.

To this criticism, Dawson devotes many pages, defending his move in a way you might expect. Dawson says his friend assumes one should always step in line with conventions or else be thought a deserter. Against that notion, Dawson mentions great reforms that began away from city centers; he goes on to defend individual genius, invoking Thoreau and so on. All boring and conventional in my view—and totally pointless. I would answer in an entirely different way.

I would know that 'society' is a made-up concept. It doesn't really mean anything. It's just kind of a handle people use to refer to a bunch of other people. It's a blanket term, covering a lot of areas indiscriminately. It's a linguistic shotgun; you can fire it and don't really have to think much about what it hits.

Using Korzybski's Razor would lead me to pose pointed counter questions to my critic. The first question is so simple: "What do you mean by society?" If I were Dawson, I'd say "Tell me, specifically, whom I hurt by moving to the country?" Perhaps Dawson helps some people. An apartment in London will now be available for someone else. Perhaps Dawson will make a greater impact on his neighbors in the country, helping them in some ways unforeseen today. The list of possible considerations is long, but beside my main point.

The question "What do you mean by 'society'?" makes Dawson's critic think a little more about what he's saying. My guess is he stumbles around a bit. And the real objection may come out. Perhaps his objection amounts to nothing more than simple envy that he can't do the same thing.

Using the Razor, at least, gets a good line of questioning going and will help you zero in on what your critic is really objecting too. No appeals to blithe and lazy generalities like 'society' allowed.

Now, for something different, a dream...

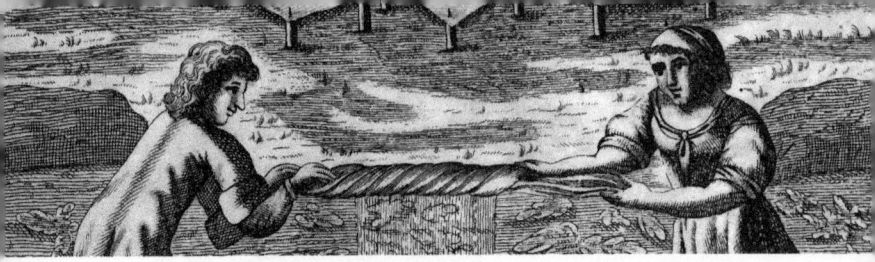

CHAPTER TWO

Interlude: Dreams

I have always had vivid dreams and an active imagination, ever since I was a young boy. Most of the time, I can't remember much of my dreams. But frequently enough, I will have dreams that are quite clear and stick with me for days as I try to sort out what they meant. I can recall bits of conversation with all kinds of people who have died long ago. Ramana Maharshi has appeared in my dreams, so real it was as if I was standing right there in hot and humid India. I could feel the sweat on my brow, I could hear the monkeys in the trees, I could smell the wood in the hall… Sometimes my dreams are just snippets of images, and sometimes I have nightmares that startle me awake.

In the summer of 2021, I had a dream that began with me standing at a site of ruins. This dream recurred, both at night and sometimes just as a daydream. And then a figure would appear and we would talk about the ruins—and a lot of other things… I wrote them down in my journal. And over the next couple of years, every now and then, new incidents and details emerged. Later I cobbled the various entries together into one series and fleshed it out a bit more and edited it. What follows, then, is part of this dream cycle. It is what Jung might call an act of active imagination. Whatever you call it, the sequence that follows grew in importance in my mind.

THE UNSPEAKABLE LEVEL

The narrative that follows seems to express some important ideas. It's a Korzybskian flight that cuts through concepts in an effort to reach that unspeakable level, a Korzybksian thirst to see through abstractions and find some unmediated experience, which is a quest perhaps as old as humanity.

What this has to do with the Razor will be more apparent after you read it. The same themes recur but expressed in a different way. Consider it an interlude. I've broken up the sequence into three interludes; they form their own little story arc within the broader book—but again the ideas are fundamental to the whole project. With that, here is the first interlude…

***

On a summer evening, I had a dream.

I stand before ruins.

Blocks of stone lay all around, as if a giant hand just brushed aside towers like toy blocks. And surrounding the ruins, a burned out forest. Nothing but blackened tree trunks and ash. The air is still and quiet, the sky gray.

Where am I? What is this?

I hear the crunch of footsteps on stony ground behind me. I turn and see a man walking toward me. He wears a long blue robe and holds a wooden staff.

"Who are you?" I call out.

I see a kind, old bearded face, grinning at me. His beard and long hair are white.

"I am one who knows himself," he says with a wink.

INTERLUDE: DREAMS

I stand confused.

He lets out a laugh. "Do not worry. It is not important just yet. But you will understand soon."

"I don't know why I am here. What is this place?"

"This is the beginning," he says.

I take an instant liking to him, something about his demeanor, his smile, his kind voice.

"The beginning always starts with destruction. It is the hardest part. To begin. But once you start, it gets..." he looks sideways thinking. "Well, not easier. But more interesting. Some find it hard to stop the destruction."

He looks over the ruins and waves his hands over them. "These were your old ideas. These were your beliefs. These were your political principles. These were your old convictions about right and wrong. Your views on how society should behave, how to work, how to... be."

He walks a little ways off toward the ruins. "Then you knocked them down. You questioned what you knew. And your old world became a desert of broken things. Come."

I follow him some distance behind the ruins. I see a small graveyard. "I see that your old heroes were properly buried," he said, again chuckling.

I look at the tombstones and see the names of people who were once important to my way of thinking: Admired authors, poets, theoreticians, business people, politicians. Famous and celebrated people. All who I once revered.

"They are dead to you now," he says. "But that is... progress of a sort."

"I did this?"

"Yes."

"How is this progress?"

"Because you cannot start on this great new beginning without killing off old long-held ideas and assumptions... They tend to get in the way," he smiled. "That you have done this much is a great credit to your start," he continued. "Yet, it is only a start. You still carry much that you will have to shed. That will be harder. For now, bask in the glory of your new beginning. You have done fine work here."

"Why did I destroy it all?"

"Because you saw through the illusions."

The old man continues:

"Your ideas of 'right' and 'wrong,' what you thought were 'good' and 'bad,' your ideas of 'success' and 'failure' 'joy' and 'sorrow'—you saw through them, saw they were—and are—and will always be—ghosts of the imagination, creations of mind.

"In the world, what 'is' is one... All concepts, ideas, divisions are imposed by the mind. They cover up 'what is' like a thick blanket of snow. All the stories you told yourself, and the stories others told you, were just that—they were stories. Different people tell different stories. But some believe that certain stories are 'true' and others 'false,' some 'good,' some 'bad.' And so they fight.

"What people fight over is a fiction..." he tapped his staff on the ground, as if to emphasize the point. "They fight over versions of their stories. They fight over arbitrary lines drawn on arbitrary maps. They fight over appearances; suffer over self-imposed fantasies; and kill over the most inconsequential of things..." He pauses, lets out a pensive "Hmm..."

"Even so, a person can find peace and happiness and freedom from that suffering. To do so, they must destroy their stories. They must knock down their own towers of stone, burn down the forest of ignorance and create their own desert," he waved expansively at the surroundings, "to start again."

He looks at me, and the gentle smile disappears. "This must be done alone. Otherwise, the dark hordes run amok...

"When people lose their myths together, the destruction and violence can be very great. The toll can be severe." Here the old fellow paused again and seemed to be recalling things that happened long ago.

"There is no path," he said finally, training his eyes back on me. "There is no place to go. The way is here." He taps his chest. "It is within you."

"Then why this place?" I ask.

"This is the beginning of your new story. You write this story. And that is why we are here."

"I am still confused."

"That is normal. Do not worry. There is more to see. And I will guide you. When you do finally see it all, you will laugh at yourself. May it be so."

The Way Out

My dreams are quiet for almost a week. And then I have another vivid dream…

I am following the old fellow on a dirt path on a ridge, grassy green hills all around, blue skies. He is wearing his blue robe peppered with silver crescent moons and yellow suns, rope belt, leather boots barely visible beneath his flowing robe and wielding his wooden staff like a walking stick.

I feel the temptation to look behind me, when he says, "Don't look back. What happened there is done and no longer exists, if it ever did. There is only the now. Everything you ever did leads to now. Come, let us follow the path."

"But you said there is no path," I say.

He doesn't answer, just keeps walking. "Don't be so literal," he says at last.

As I walk I have the sensation of forgetting something important. I reach into my pockets. No phone, no wallet.

"You won't need them," he says without turning around. It all seems quite surreal.

"Am I dreaming again?"

"How do you know you are dreaming?"

"Because this place—"

"—is not real?" He stops and looks at me with that warm smile. "What does that mean?"

I find myself struggling for words. "Is it not obvious? This is not my life. I don't know where I am."

"How does it matter?"

I want to say "Isn't it obvious?" But I know in my heart what he says is hard to answer. It is not easy to say what is real and what is not. Or rather, it is not easy to prove. Am I dreaming? I must be. Isn't it obvious?

"It's never obvious," he says, seeming to read my thoughts. "Never. Or more people would see it."

"See what?"

"The veil of ignorance that covers everything, that makes everyday concerns seem so real and important. All that wanting and striving… When you pierce the veil, you will begin to question the sanity of everyone else. And if you are not quiet about it, they will begin to question yours."

"I have had that feeling. I have thought to myself more than once, 'What are people doing? Who would organize the world this way?' It is insane."

"Yes, but to call the world names will not help you. You have to accept it as it is, even welcome it. Everything is exactly as it must be, as it can only be, given what has happened already."

"That is a hard teaching."

"Waking up never happens without it."

We continue to walk along the dirt path. We have moved far beyond the blackened forest and those toppled towers. The landscape is stunningly beautiful all around… green mountains and valleys that roll on seemingly forever and white puffy clouds overhead against a deep blue sky.

The landscape and fresh air and sunshine seem to make my daily affairs especially distant.

We come to a copse of trees.

"Let's rest here," the old man says. We sit under the cooling shade of the trees.

"I feel at peace here," I say, "even though I don't know why I'm here..."

"There doesn't have to be a reason, not one we have to know anyway. Not everything happens for a reason. Things just happen."

"Yes, you remind me of something one of my favorite thinkers said. He said that everything happens, in the same way as rain falls from the clouds or as snow melts under the rays of the sun or as dust rises with the wind. These things just happen."

"Gurdjieff," the old man says, and I am not surprised he knows.

"Yes..."

He nods. "A wise fellow, even if a bit of a rascal."

"I've learned some things from him."

"I know," he says. "Cause and effect are an illusion. He knew it. Things happen. Everything just happens. It's all one movement. To say one thing causes another thing makes no more sense than to say night causes day. Things just happen. That is all we can say."

"So, I feel like this is a dream, my meetings with you."

He nods his head as if I was sort of right. "In a sense, yes... but that shouldn't make any of it less real. Everything you experience is, in a sense, an act of imagination... You make the world; it doesn't exist apart from you. It is hard to explain."

"I don't feel like I make the world," I say.

"Well, not literally," he says with a shrug.

"The whole world is so confusing... Why does anybody do anything?"

"Or maybe nobody does anything. Or maybe," he pauses again, "things just happen."

"Why does it seem like I am on a lonely quest?"

"Because the quest is not easy and one must look deep into oneself. Most people don't want to see themselves. They are afraid of what they might see. And those who do look, often don't like what they see. Hence, the distractions... the toys of civilization... They help numb the pain. Then one does not have to look at oneself. Nobody wants to knock over their own towers, as you have done. That was a big step."

"Why me, I wonder? Why didn't I just be like everyone else and..."

"Stay asleep?" he offers.

"Yes."

He looks off on the horizon. "I can't say."

"You can't say?"

"No... It is one of those mysteries. But I will say, you are not as alone as you think. And many came before you. You know some of them already. You have studied their works and lives. They are the great wise spirits, the sages of human history... Those who pierced the veil, who saw. Those who woke up. And there are many others that no one ever hears about."

"I am determined to be one of them, though I know that seems very arrogant to say."

"You are already one of them. There is nothing to achieve, nothing to realize."

"I am astonished and encouraged by your words! And I enjoy your company. I am glad I knocked over my own towers. But I feel there is more to explore and that I am not quite there."

"Likewise," he says, smiling. "There are some very interesting encounters ahead—not just with me. But I will be with you, for I am your guide—and much more." He has that twinkle in his eyes again and a warm smile.

The Book

Days pass and soon another dream...

We come to a small, square stone cottage with a pitched roof. The old man motions for me to have a look. There is no door and we walk right in. There is only a single room, stained glass windows, light shining upon a free-standing book easel where a book lay open.

"Take a look," he says, standing aside.
I walk up and read the following out loud:

> Striving and craving,
> For pleasure or prosperity,
> These are your enemies...

> Let them all go.
> Hold on to nothing.

> Every good fortune,
> Wives, friends, houses, lands,
> All these gifts and riches...

> They are a dream
> A juggling act,
> A traveling show!

> A few days, and they are gone!

> Desire binds you,
> Nothing else.
> Destroy it and you are free.

I stop and do not turn the page.
"I have read this before..." I say. "It is from *The Ashtavakra Gita*. These passages express an idea, often repeated in the great wise books, about finding freedom in the absence of desire."

INTERLUDE: DREAMS

I turn to the old man and say: "It seems right, if a bit harsh. And easy to say... Living it is much harder, perhaps not possible."

"Don't give up so easily," he says. "Have you tried to live those words?"

"To an extent, yes. I don't want many, or most, of the things my fellow humans find so alluring. I don't care for fancy clothes, expensive cars, or big homes. I don't crave titles or power or fame. I like to have money, certainly, enough to guarantee a certain lifestyle and independence—but I don't have any special craving or desire to get rich."

"That is quite a lot to give up."

"But it is not the entire list... Even if I say I would be happy to live a quiet life of contemplation and reading, that is itself a desire. Even so modest a desire as a wish for good health, or simple absence of physical pain is, still, a desire...

"And you don't think you can overcome these desires?" he says as he raises an eyebrow.

"I must say, it seems unlikely... But I wonder, when these teachings require one act so contrary to nature. Why should existence be such a fight? Why not live more in harmony with the way we are?"

"And what way is that? Is there such a thing as human nature?"

"Maybe not," I say, "but birds do not give up flying; lions don't give up meat and fish don't climb trees. They fulfill the nature that comes easily to them. Why shouldn't humans do the same? Why all this fuss over how to live?"

"Birds don't worship abstractions of their own creation, lions don't build nuclear bombs and fish don't write books. Human beings are different. Remember your Korzybski."

I am, again, not surprised he brings up Korzybski. He seems to know what I've read, what I've thought.

"Yes, old Korzybski was right," I say. "Humans are time-binders." Time-binding is a central idea in Korzybski's thought. Essentially, time-binding is how we transmit knowledge across time. We can read the words of Aristotle and Spinoza, Darwin and Einstein. We have the ability to pass on complex ideas across many generations. These plans and recipes, a treasury of know-how and experience, we use and improve and pass on. We are, in Korzybski's words, both an "inheritor of the by-gone ages and the trustee of posterity."

"And time-binding," the old man says, "creates, in part, the human situation."

"And that human situation is... natural."

"Exactly," he says. "The fuss, as you called it, is very human, part of what it means to be human... Human beings fuss over how to live. It is their special thing. So, you have to play the game, whether you want to or not. The only question is: How will you play it?"

"The *Gita* points to a way..."

"Do not give up on it," he says. "Make it your life's work."

We walk out of the cottage and back on the dirt track road. "The world seems a very strange thing," I say. "It doesn't seem to make sense."

"What is 'sense' but a human idea?"

"True," I admit. "Everything is just as it is. We create distinctions, draw lines, seek structure and order, and try to gain an understanding of what is going on. But our means may be flawed. What we think we know may well turn out to be an illusion."

"It has often been the case," he adds, "that what people believe to be true, later people decide is untrue."

I nod in agreement. "It makes it difficult to be dogmatic on any point of consequence... and yet many are so certain."

"Certainty makes people comfortable; too much uncertainty drives them mad," he says.

I continue: "Once you see through it—once you topple your own towers of beliefs and burn your forests of ignorance—you can't unsee it... I can never go back. I will forever see all concepts and ideas as human constructions, as sort of unreal... One even comes to see the 'I' itself as a construction... and the thought 'I do this' and 'I do that' are just powerful illusions, the idea that 'I am that' or 'I am this' become absurd... That is not to say there is nothing, there is something behind the veil of words and concepts, the unspeakable level as Korzybski called it... Even so, I can't help but wonder about awareness itself."

"What do you wonder about it?"

"I wonder... where it came from? How did it start?"

"Those, too, are human concepts," he reminds me. "Perhaps there is no beginning or end, there is no from or to, no time at all."

"I suspect you may be on the right track—there I go again; what is 'right' exactly? I ask rhetorically, and expect no answer... I take comfort in the old wisdom of the *Ashtavakra Gita*. Know yourself in all things, and in all things see your own self. 'The wise man knows the Self, and he plays the game of life. But the fool lives in the world like a beast of burden.' As I have said, it is a hard teaching…"

"The *Gita* says it is easy."

"I love that the *Gita* says it is easy. It certainly sounds simple. But somehow it isn't easy, even if you believe the teaching is 'right'… I am not sure it is."

"Perhaps doubt holds you back?" the old man looks at me askance with that raised eyebrow.

"I can't help but doubt. How can one stop questioning? I never understand 'believers' who take something as 'true'–and stop… I agree, someone with no doubts might have less trouble with these questions; but I would also say they never get past shallow ground, never really know themselves.. "

"Yes. Your doubts are pointers to where you should work, where treasures lie. As you step through various encounters of your imagination, you will dig there. But you know a lot more than you think and you stand on much firmer ground than you give it credit for. Doubt as you will, you will feel your way to foundations on which to build a happy, contented life."

Under a Tree

Another night, another dream…

The old man and I are relaxing under the shade of a tree, once again, with a spectacular view of the valley below...

He starts: "Desires. We can agree this is the crux of the whole thing. Happiness might be defined as the absence of desire."

"Maybe. Can happiness reside in wanting something? It seems impossible. Not wanting a thing would seem to entail complete equanimity, peace, happiness... whatever you want to call it. A state of being beyond pain, suffering and injury of any sort..."

"And the dead?" he asks me.

"The dead have no desires, so they would seem happy... and yet that doesn't make sense. The dead have no awareness, so far as we know. They have ceased to exist as individual 'I's' in this world, so there is no capacity to experience desire."

"Then it would seem this happy state requires absence of desire... yet, also the capacity for it." He's prodding me along.

"Maybe. Kind of like, if you never wanted a thing to begin with, its loss can't really be called a sacrifice. To go without desire really means to have desire sublimated into a feeling of letting go."

"To be thirsty and yet decline a drink," he says, merrily, "... and not miss it in any way. Is that possible?"

"That may be possible. Rather than saying no desire at all, which I thought might be impossible for a living human being... We can say 'to sublimate desire' instead. Toward a letting go, a willing release, with no regrets... Which may be sophistry, old man. Am I not again elevating a 'desire to be without desire' above desire itself?"

He nods. "I think maybe you twist yourself into knots of words unnecessarily. Forget the words. Think of the doing. It is possible to be as you described. Think about it."

"I agree. I think of the great sage Ramana Maharshi. There is a 'real man' who lived in the modern age, the world of TVs and airplanes and world wars, and he seemed to be as free of desire and as full of peace and equanimity as one can imagine... A flesh and blood man, of which we have photos and ample testimony from those who spent time with him, lived with him. And never have I read a word that showed the great man as anything other than the great man he was reported to be. Truly astounding."

"He was a true master of life," the old man agrees. "And so it can be done... I would also bring to your attention the words of St. Gregory of Nyssa. He said desires were like the threat of a spider's web and just as a spider's web can be easily swept away with the swipe of a hand, so too those desires can be shoved aside.

"Here is St. Gregory," and the old man clears his throat and begins:

> 'All that man pursues in this life has no existence except in his mind, not in reality: opinion, honor, dignities, glory, fortune: all these are the work of this life's spiders... But those who rise to the heights escape, with the flick of a wing, from the spiders of this world. Only those who, like flies, are heavy and without energy remain caught in the glue of this world and are taken and bound, as though in nets, by honors, pleasures, praise and manifold desires, and thus they become the prey of the beast that seeks to capture them.'

"That is nice, is it not?" he says smiling at me.

"That is quite good... and very poetic. I have never read that before. Wonderful. All these sages seem to know the way."

"And they say it can be done. In fact, they have done it."

INTERLUDE: DREAMS

"They have. And so why can't I?"

And so I close out the first set of visions. They cover much of the same ground we have gone over to this point in explaining the Razor. We have increased our awareness of abstractions—and we have a mode, or means or system, to question them, to poke at them, to pull them back and see what lies underneath, to stretch for that unspeakable level. These probings can go as deep as you'd like.

For the next chapter, we'll go back to a more conventional exposition as we explore another aspect of abstractions; the idea of polarities...

CHAPTER THREE

Polarities

Here we spend some time with one of the fundamental laws of our universe; an insight that Korzybski's Razor readily reveals and one I've hinted at already. The idea is again simple yet profound. And it is one appreciated by many of the sages of history.

In this chapter, we delve into the world of polarity.

***

"What, exactly, is polarity? It is something much more than simple duality or opposition. For to say that opposites are polar is to say much more than they are far apart; it is to say they are related and joined—that they are the terms, ends, or extremities of a single whole. Polar opposites are therefore inseparable opposites."

–Alan Watts, *Two Hands of God*

"The road up and the road down are the same thing."

–Heraclitus (535–475 BC)

***

orzybski admits to being "baffled... for many years," as he notes in the introduction to *Science and Sanity*, by the fact that humans from all kinds of times and places have some set of either/or evaluations: day or night, land or water, life or death, hot or cold, capitalism or communism, democrat or republican, etc. "And so on endlessly on all levels," as he says.

Yet, the world in which we walk and breathe is not nearly so tidy. There are degrees of nuance between these either/or constructions, but additionally, each pole is defined by the existence of its opposite. In fact, the poles are connected. In a sense they are one. This observation is obvious but often forgotten and is one we will explore more here.

Polarity is one of the great principles of the universe, as Chuang-Tzu said (as quoted by Watts in *The Two Hands of God: The Myths of Polarity*): "Those who would have right without its correlative, wrong; or good government without its correlative, misrule— they do not apprehend the great principles of the universe nor the conditions to which all creation is subject."

There is no escaping this principle. Whatever concept you can think of *must* have its opposite. (I'm going to let this slide without a formal proof. Perhaps you can imagine something that does not have an opposite. For example, what is the opposite of the color blue? But even here we could say there is 'blue' and there is 'the opposite of blue'—which feels like playing word games. More practically we could say blue is a color and the opposite of any color is no color at all. Either way, I don't find this discussion all that interesting or important, and so I move on...)

Thus these concepts are inseparable from each other. They are polar. There is no sense of light unless there is also darkness. There is no up without down. And so on.

There are many such combinations we could think of:

Free will and determinism
Good and evil
Natural and unnatural
Faith and reason
Subjective and objective
Pleasure and pain
Remembering vs. forgetting
Love and hate
Virtues and vices
Truth and falsehood

Poverty and riches
Male and female
Strong and weak
Youth and old age
Heaven and hell
Sleep and wakefulness
Bravery and cowardice

This reminds me of the famous "table of opposites," preserved by Aristotle in his *Metaphysics*, in which he lists pairs such as male and female, left and right, straight and crooked, etc.

Polarities, or the notion of opposites, played an important role in the thinking of bygone eras. And for some wise souls, polarity was an idea to surpass, or overcome. By doing this, you achieved a sort of enlightenment.

For example, consider Meister Eckhart...

The Way of Paradox

"I have called Eckhart's way 'the way of Paradox,' because he sees the Reality of God as something that can be grasped only within the tension and clash of opposites."

—Cyprian Smith,
 The Way of Paradox: Spiritual Life as Taught by Meister Eckhart

Meister Eckhart was one of the greatest of Christian mystics. He died in 1328, but his works have gone on to influence many thinkers ever since, among them Carl Jung, Alan Watts, and Martin Heidegger. Eckhart has proven popular with those who see connections between 'eastern' ways of thinking (such as Buddhism and Hindu Vedanta) and the 'western' mystics. For example, D.T. Suzuki wrote about "the closeness of Meister Eckhart's way of thinking to that of Mahāyāna Buddhism, especially of Zen Buddhism."

It is easy to see such connections when reading Eckhart, especially with his talk about detachment (*gelassenheit*) and "the humble man and God are one and not two," among other ideas. In one of his sermons, Eckhart says, "When I preach, it is my wont to speak about detachment, and of how man should rid himself of self and all things." Which would have many Buddhists nodding their head in agreement.

Eckhart has wide appeal partly because he seems non-dogmatic and because he draws on many traditions. *The Complete Mystical Sermons of Meister Eckhart* can be read with pleasure today; the sermons are often short, include his personal reflections, and were written in the vernacular and hence are more accessible than his theological treatises written in Latin.

As Cyprian Smith tells us, Eckhart drew from the Bible and Christian authors, as you would expect, but also from 'Pagan,' Jewish and Arab sources. Eckhart even drew from the Béguines, Friends of God, Brethren of the Free Spirit, which were marginal movements, even heretical. They all seemed to have taught him something, Smith writes. Eckhart's unorthodox style would eventually get him in trouble with the Pope and the ecclesiastical authorities of his time. He would die before they could get to him.

Most important for our immediate purposes: Eckhart grasped the centrality of opposites and sought to see through them, to see their connectedness. He saw all opposites, or contraries, as contained in a unity, which he saw as God: "pleasure and pain, success and failure, are all ultimately one in God," Smith writes in his *The Way of Paradox*. (Nicholas of Cusa, an influential polymath of the 14th century and who was influenced by Eckhart, would come to describe God as a *coincidentia oppositorum*, a unity of opposites.)

Eckhart keeps that tension alive in his writings; to lose sight of it is to lose sight of the fundamental reality of our existence. 'Truth' lies not in affirming it or denying it, but in surpassing it—seeing truth as lying "in the tug-of-war between the two [opposites]."

In this way, Eckhart's 'God' surpasses descriptions. Our opposites are human constructions, and therefore God is not any of them. He cannot be good or wise or powerful ("He" cannot even be a "he"); those are human ideas. And they have opposites. Hence, Eckhart rejects such limited depictions. God is beyond these concepts, an ultimate reality with no name—which, nonetheless, Eckhart refers to as the root, the ground, the source. We might more generally speak of reality, or 'what is' as not being our descriptions of it, but as lying beyond them. Our unspeakable level.

"Eckhart's spiritual way," Smith writes, "is a way of paradox, antithesis. Two apparently opposed realities will be brought by him into clashing confrontation, until the dualism separating them is transcended and their underlying unity emerges like sunlight after rain." Eckhart describes this transcendent power as "neither *this* nor *that*." It is free of names and forms, unanchored to our verbal conceptions. (Again, this sounds like the unspeakable level…)

Similarly, what we call "I" and "you" are projections, images, concepts… and when we roll them back, we see that beautiful underlying unity again with all things. As Eckhart says, "I am not my body, nor my mind, nor my emotions, nor am I all these things taken together. So what am I? What is 'me'?"

Smith describes this self in terms Ramana Maharshi would recognize: detached, tranquil, serene:

> It is never excited about anything, never downcast or depressed by anything. It is like a deep, perhaps even bottomless, lake; my various thoughts and emotions are like ripples or waves upon the surface. But below the surface, in the depth, there are no ripples; everything is still. Strange fish live there, and feathery fronds of aquatic plants. Once the turbulence on the surface has died down and the water becomes quite clear, we can see into the depths and become aware of what lives there. But even this is not the lake itself; it is not me. 'I' am that which contains it all, the water which is still water, whether it is calm or ruffled,

fresh or salt, thronged with fish or totally empty. This is the true, the permanent self.

Here, one is utterly unmoved by emotions and untroubled by thoughts, free of opposites. One no longer worries about what happened in the past, one no longer frets about what may happen in the future—for again, these are concepts, opposites to be transcended. There is no why, there is no purpose, there is no aim; one just is. You become one with the rhythm of the Universe, the rhythm inherent in things, as Smith says; the breathing in and breathing out, birth and death, growth and decline, gain and loss, like the changing of the seasons, they are a whole—a single symphonic piece.

To get to this state, as Smith writes, one must simply be still: "relaxed, free, spontaneous, untroubled, open to the present moment and whatever it contains."

In my own copy of Eckhart's mystical sermons, I highlighted this from Sermon 14, which echoes the Stoics: "You should be firm and steadfast; that is, you should be the same in weal and woe, in fortune and misfortune, having the noble nature of precious stones..."

And earlier he makes it clear there is no 'other,' no 'dualisms'; whatever is received in the vessel, the vessel is in it also, and is the vessel itself. "That which embraces is that which is embraced, for it embraces nothing but itself. This is subtle. He who understands it has been preached to long enough."

Eckhart was influenced by an earlier thinker who had similar ideas: Pseudo-Dionysius.

Pseudo-Dionysius: Naming What Can't Be Named

It has taken me a while to figure out the role of Pseudo-Dionysius in all of this. I bought a book of his collected works years ago, mostly because of Alan Watts. Watts translated Pseudo-Dionysius's book *On Divine Names* and respected his ideas as important. That was enough to get my curiosity going.

Pseudo-Dionysius for several centuries was thought to be the 'actual' Dionysisus referred to in the Book of Acts: the first Athenian convert of St. Paul. That identity was decisively debunked, but his wide influence did not diminish.

When I first tried to read this book, I did not get far. But I kept the book nonetheless. My intuition told me this book could yet have a role to play. And so it has proven to be. As my own thinking led me on a path seeking to transcend opposites, reconcile them, mediate them, dissolve them, unify them, attend to that unspeakable level... I kept bumping into Pseudo-Dionysius again and again.

Pseudo-Dionysius' importance lies in his insistence on the limitations of our language and concepts. For him, the ultimate divinity was simply unknowable. He would have agreed with the later author of *The Cloud of Unknowing* when asked about 'God':

> "But now you put me a question and say: 'How might I think of him myself, and what is he?' And to this I can only answer thus: 'I have no idea.'"

Yet, Pseudo-Dionysius was not silent. God is a unity of opposites, of everything. This Unity is itself beyond words. Dionysius describes that unity as the inscrutable One, the inexpressible One, the Source of all Unity, the Nameless One. "With a wise silence, we do honor to the inexpressible." He writes:

> How then can we speak of the divine names? How can we do this if the Transcendent surpasses all discourse and all knowledge, if it abides beyond the reach of the mind and of being, if it encompasses and circumscribes, embraces and

anticipate all things while itself eluding their grasp and escaping from any perception, imagination, opinion, name, discourse, apprehension, or understanding?

That is the challenge: How to speak of the state that transcends opposites without invoking the same dualities all over again? It may be hard or even impossible to express in words and images. But it can be felt. Pseudo-Dionysius points to the way and then you must feel it for yourself.

I do not intend to provide a synopsis on the thought of Pseudo-Dionysius, which can be as obscure and enigmatic as it is alluring. I merely want to note him as an influential fellow traveler in recognizing the difficulty of trying to surpass the limitations of language and the world of polarities.

Moreover, his apophatic theology was an attempt to deal with these challenges, which had a great impact on many later thinkers. It is also quite compatible with Korzybski's idea of "whatever you say a thing is, it is not."

Nirdvandva: **Freedom From Opposites**

Out beyond ideas of wrongdoing
   and rightdoing
There is a field. I'll meet you there.

—Rumi (quoted in Challenger)

Let's move along in our exploration of opposites; seeing their connections, seeing them as human ideas, as something that need not bind us, as something one can go beyond. I find it hard to express exactly what this means. But I am in good company. Many before me have struggled with the "problem of opposites."

For Carl Jung, the idea was of central importance. In *Psychological Types*, Jung writes about *The Laws of Manu*, a Hindu text of uncertain age which represents itself as a discourse of Manu. Jung points out that there is a Sanskrit word for "pairs of opposites," *dvandva*. What is particularly interesting about this word is it can also mean strife or conflict. Per the The Laws of Manu, the world-creator ordained *dvandva*:

> ...in order to distinguish actions, he separated merit from demerit, and he caused the creatures to be affected by the pairs of opposites, such as pain and pleasure.

Jung comments: "As further pairs of opposites, the commentator Kulluka names desire and anger, love and hate, hunger and thirst, care and folly, honor and disgrace. The *Ramayana* says: 'This world must suffer under the pairs of opposites forever.' Not to allow oneself to be influenced by the pairs of opposites, but to be *nirdvandva* (free, untouched by the opposites), to raise oneself above them, is an essentially ethical task, because deliverance from opposites leads to redemption."

Here we see this freedom from opposites—which amounts to a kind of seeing through them—as being associated with freedom from suffering.

Manu says:

> Then [in the deepest meditation, *samadhi*] comes the state of being untroubled by the opposites...

And again, in terms very much in line with Eckhart:

> He who remains the same in living as in dying, in fortune as in misfortune, whether gaining or losing, loving or hating, will be liberated.

I try to imagine some concrete way in which such liberation may become a practical reality, in part by reflecting on my own life as I have integrated polarities into my thinking. For one thing, I find I have lost my taste for arguing with people over polarities, such as debating over whether or not we have free will, for example. I see both as human constructs that need each other: Ergo, there cannot be "free will" alone or "determinism" alone for these concepts to make any sense, just as there must be light to know darkness and up to know down. There must be both. Or better, neither, as both may be phantoms of the mind. To surpass these opposites altogether would be to see the world without either, as something not quite captured by either of these concepts.

Similarly, what is natural versus unnatural? Environmentally sensitive people criticize humanity for altering the environment in destructive ways. But all animals alter their environment. Such criticisms put (some) human activity outside of what is natural. I can't accept such dualisms any longer; it is all one thing. (What people usually mean when they call something 'unnatural' is that they don't like it. What they like, they call 'natural.')

So, too, with attempts to be 'objective' versus 'subjective.' There are no such things. A person's views on any matter are their own views. It is impossible to get outside one's own point of view. These adjectives of 'objective' and 'subjective' no longer come into play for me.

I also take fortunes and misfortunes with more circumspection. For example, in terms of successes and setbacks in my business, I see events unfolding as they must. The very ideas of 'success' or a 'setback' are my own imposition on what happened. I take such things with a great deal of humility. As I mentioned earlier, an apparent success may unlock an unfortunate future event; and an apparent setback may set the stage for a later success. One simply never knows. But one can know the polarity of these things, which is to say the necessity of both.

To see both is to see contrasts and recognize them as the roots of experience and judgment. For example, I play golf and will sometimes think after a very bad round how I needed to have this round to appreciate the really good rounds. The polarity is necessary. There are no good shots without bad shots.

To be free of both is to recognize these categories as human concepts—and to be the ultimate Zen golfer, unphased by 'poor shots' and happy to simply play. In the world out there, as it is, there is no difference between 'good shots' and 'bad shots.' We make the judgment of what constitutes a good shot and a bad shot. Polarities force us to confront such judgments, see through them and, perhaps, achieve some peace and calm as a result.

As an aside, I've used this phrase "see through them" a handful of times. In thinking more about what this means, Alan Watts perhaps had it right when he wrote in his book *Psychotherapy East and West*: "It cannot be stated too strongly that liberation does not involve the destruction of such conventional concepts as ego; it means *seeing through them*—in the same way that we can use the idea of the equator without confusing it with a physical mark upon the surface of the earth." Ergo, our zen golfer cannot win or lose because such concepts mean nothing to him; "he has nothing to prove and nothing to defend," as Watts puts it.

Resolving opposites solves other problems that seem to vex people. If you go around believing in an all-powerful 'God' who can only be good, for example, then you have a hard time dealing with the horrible things that happen to good and innocent people. I don't need to rehash here the usual age-old 'problem of evil' and the contradictions inherent in an all-powerful God. (See, for example, Epicurus' Trilemma.) But the contradictions are age-old because there is no good resolution except to see 'good' and 'evil' as human concepts with no existence outside of human minds whatsoever.

As I mentioned, the problem of opposites features prominently in Jung's thought. (It is a central concern of *The Red Book*.) One place where he addresses this is in his lectures on the spiritual exercises of Ignatius of Loyola, published in a careful and lovely edition by the Philemon Foundation. I didn't pick this book up because of any particular interest in Loyola, but because I'm interested in Jung. And in the course of his discussion, Jung visits this subject of the problem of opposites.

In Lecture 4, he gets to the idea of opposites and how 'Christian' thinkers typically differ from 'Eastern' ones. As he says, the attitude of 'western people' is to overcome, or conquer desire and 'win.' We want to avoid suffering entirely and seek pleasure. By contrast, he says, the attitude of 'eastern people' is to seek liberation from pleasure *and* pain; to escape the opposites entirely. "One frees oneself not only from the bad," Jung writes, "but also from the good. One frees oneself from these two, becomes *nirdvandva*: that is free of opposites."

Such divisions as 'east' and 'west' are not strictly accurate, or even necessary. We have traditions in 'the west' that mirror these 'eastern' concerns. They are simply not as well known. But let us pass over that for a moment; the general point stands about differing attitudes toward pleasure and pain, whatever we choose to call such attitudes.

Jung quotes extensively from the works of Erich Przywara (1889-1972), a philosopher and theologian, and favors his interpretation of Christ as being a union or conciliation of opposites. Mankind is "a central meeting point, a meeting point of great cosmic opposites. The human being is a kind of uniting symbol; man in this form corresponds in a way to God as a prototype, or rather a copy, in which all opposites are also unified in God."

Here again, we hear echoes of Eckhart. "The cross," he goes on to say, "is the symbol for the uniting of opposites, and Christ vanquishes the opposites. In him, opposites are overcome."

This may strike you as a rather uncommon view of Christ. But it is not so unusual among Christian mystics[1], where God is the unity of all things—including opposites. In the Gospel of Thomas, Jesus himself extols the union of opposites as an entrance to the Kingdom of Heaven:

When you make the two one, and when you make the inside like the outside, and the outside like the inside, and the above like the below, and when you make the male and female one and the same, so that the male not be male and the female female... then you will enter the kingdom.

It should go without saying that you don't have to be a Christian or believer to engage in these ideas. Whatever your religious beliefs (or lack thereof), they remain excellent illustrations of humans grappling with the problem of opposites.

Later, in Lecture 8, Jung cites the alchemist Gerhard Dorn (1530-1584). Lest you dismiss alchemy as a discredited and foolhardy attempt to turn lead into gold, I will point out that alchemy was a practice that involved laboratory work but deals mostly with trying to discover the hidden order and essence of things, and the transformation of the physical and the spiritual. The work of alchemists left us with a rich treasury of images and enigmatic texts. Reading through some of the classics of the genre will quickly disabuse you of any notion you may have of alchemy as some frivolous fraud. On the contrary, the best of the alchemists₁ (subscript here denoting they were not all the same; undoubtedly there were fraudsters) pursued alchemy as a serious subject and inquiry. One can spend hours contemplating the images alone, complex in meaning and telling a story of transformation all their own. (The images of the Mutus Liber that salt the pages of this book tell one such story.)

If you are ever in Amsterdam, I would recommend a visit to the Embassy of the Free Mind, a museum which houses thousands of old alchemical and hermetic texts, full of

Atalanta Fugiens, 1618

such images. On my last visit, I picked up a postcard with the nearby image of the two eagles. It is from *Atalanta Fugiens*, a classic of the genre, published in 1618. The caption on the back of the postcard reads: "Two eagles meet, one from the East, the other from the West. They become one, representing the union of opposites in the creation of the Philosopher's Stone."

Alchemists were mindful of opposites, and Jung was an enthusiastic student of alchemy. He wrote in his *Mysterium Coniunctionis*: "The tremendous role which the opposites and their union play in alchemy helps us understand why the alchemists were so fond of paradoxes. In order to attain this union, they tried not only to visualize the opposites together but to express them in the same breath." Hence, images of hermaphrodites and the conjunction of the sun and moon, among many others. Alchemists saw the world as separated, but sought ways to unify the whole.

Nearby, you'll see an image of a *rebis*, another image symbolizing the union of opposites. Here we have male and female united, but there are other tropes used as well. The gold wing symbolizes the sun; the blue wing, the moon. Red and white, too, traditionally represent opposites. We will see more of these images later in the book.

Dorn points out that "on the second day of creation God created the binarius—the dyad—when he separated the upper and lower waters." This separation represents the creation of opposites, the source of

A Rebis, Symbolizing the Union of Opposites

mankind's confusions and illusions. "The binarius separates, it destroys [the prior unity]" Jung writes. "That is why the second day of creation is the only day on which God did not say, 'It is good.'"

Good and evil were born that day, so the story goes. And that split is resolved in the concept of God. He is, as Jung says, "the *coincidentia oppositorum*, the coming together of the opposites, the resolution of all opposites and the release from them." (A footnote includes a fun word to express opposites: "Doppelheit" which means "duality.")

We are creatures of conflict and doubt because "we hang between the opposites"– and in this hanging, we are analogous to the suffering Christ–so goes the Przywara interpretation.

These ideas all say much about why we can get so confused. As mentioned above: How do we reconcile the existence of 'evil' with the idea of an all-powerful and 'good' God? People have twisted themselves in all kinds of knots over the question because they did not want to face the obvious fact that these opposites require each other; you cannot have 'good' without 'evil.' They are concepts and thus the source, God, gods, Nature, whatever, must then contain both of them or surpass them. They are necessary polarities.

'Life' and 'death'? Polarities. We cannot have one without the other. Why see death, then, as something so terrible? It is what gives life meaning. Without death there can be no life.

What about 'victory' and 'defeat'? Polarities. There must be both wins and losses.

There cannot be any one quality without its opposite: No happiness without the sadness; not here without a there; no inside without outside; no belief without unbelief; no freedom without unfreedom; no profit without loss; they are all of a piece. The grand project of self-enlightenment demands reconciliation of opposites and achieving a state of *nirdvandva*.

Once you start seeing the world this way, everything changes. And in ways you will not like—at least not initially. I would explore more of these ways later. But for now, the important first step was to see this necessity of opposites and to understand, at a deeper level, that the only way out of our confusions and conflicts is to resolve these opposites, to bring them together again.

Korzybski's Razor was a footstool in helping me reach these ideas. The Razor casts such grand concepts as 'good' and 'evil' off their thrones. They are merely words, made by humans. Once I saw that, truly saw it, I could see polarities clear as day and, in particular, the folly of many arguments.

I have often felt that the world's wisest sages all end up in the same sort of place. They use different language and rely on different cultural motifs and stories, but they all come around to a message that is remarkably similar, from Parmenides to Buddha, a breaking down of human concepts, a dissolution of the idea of a personal ego and a recognition of a broader and deeper self that encompasses and connects all things and experiences.

CHAPTER FOUR

Who Is This 'I'?

Near the end of the last chapter, I used the phrase "dissolution of the idea of a personal ego." In this chapter, we'll take a deeper look at the idea of self. I also mentioned earlier that seeing the world through the lens I am presenting may change things for you in ways you might not like initially. The conclusion below is one of the changes in worldview I had in mind.

But press and see what you think, for there is a happy ending after all.

***

"It is all one vast awakened thing.
I call it the golden eternity. It is perfect.
We were never really born, we will never really die.
It has nothing to do with the imaginary idea of a
personal self, other selves, many selves everywhere:
Self is only an idea, a mortal idea."

–Jack Kerouac (wielding the Razor)

***

In October 2023, I headed to the Players Club in New York City to attend a symposium hosted by the Institute of General Semantics. I gave a talk on the nature of self, which I titled "Who Is This 'I'?"

I opened with a question: When you say 'I,' what does that identity entail? In other words: What do you think of when you think of yourself?

Korzybski gives us a great tool we can use to think about this question: the chain index, which has always fascinated me. The chain index is the idea that a thing is not identical to itself in different space-times. My iphone$_{\text{in New York City}}$ is not the same as my iphone$_{\text{in my house}}$. This is a fact that might not matter most of the time, but it can matter. For example, at home, my cellular coverage is not as strong, so I use wi-fi, whereas in New York City—with the "same phone"—I rely on my cellular service. And that affects how the phone works and performs.

The implications of the chain index, though, are much deeper when you apply them to yourself, or to people generally. The chain index teaches you that you are not identical to yourself in different settings. You are not the same person at work as you are at home. You are not the same person when you are with friends as you are in the quiet of your own study. You exist as an organism-as-a-whole-in-its-environment, as Korzybski would say, an insight that blurs the edges of the self. Where do "you" begin and where do "you" end? And when?

We tend to think of ourselves as "skin encapsulated egos," as Alan Watts used to say. But even insides *need* their outsides. You need a place to stand, air to breathe, and so on. You also have a history, a history of things that had to happen exactly as they did for you to be here at all. You had to have parents, and your parents had to have parents. And so if you follow this train of thought long enough, you find that you invoke the entire universe. (Remember Carl Sagan's quip, about baking an apple pie from scratch. You must first create the universe.) Everything is connected to everything else. You are different, but are you truly separate?

The chain index makes the environment part of the defining feature of a "self"—you can't extract it or separate it. They are so tightly connected and bound as to be one thing.

Korzybski himself didn't seem to explore this aspect of the chain index, but there are instances where he gave definite hints. In *Science and Sanity*, he writes:

> Einstein realized that the empirical structure of 'space' and 'time' with which the physicist and the average man deals is such that it cannot be empirically divided, and that we actually deal with a blend which we have split only elementalistically and verbally into these fictitious entities.

I would emphasize that phrase "fictitious entities." Would the idea of a "self" be a fictitious entity?

What's interesting here, too, is that Einstein definitely saw the more radical implications of this idea of organism-as-a-whole-in-its-environment. I am reminded of my favorite Einstein quote, which appears in a 1950 letter to a rabbi named Robert S. Marcus:

> A human being is part of the whole, called by us 'Universe'; a part limited in time and space. He experiences himself, his thoughts and feelings as something separated from the rest—a kind of optical delusion of his consciousness. This delusion is a kind of prison for us, restricting us to our personal desires and affection for a few persons nearest us. Our task must be to free ourselves from this prison by widening our circle of compassion to embrace all living

creatures and the whole of nature in its beauty. Nobody is able to achieve this completely but striving for such achievement is, in itself, a part of the liberation and a foundation for inner security.

So here, he clearly states the self has blurry edges, and he sees its connection to everything else. I also like the strong words "delusion" and "prison."

But for now, we return to Korzybski: Most of the time, when he's talking about organisms as a whole in their environment, he's not talking about people per se, but about other organisms; for example, at one point in *Science and Sanity* there is an extended discussion of jellyfish. When he talks about people, he's more interested in empirical facts about them and their actions. But there are times when he comes close to Einstein, as he does here in *Science and Sanity*:

> All forms of human activities are interconnected. It is impossible to select a special characteristic and treat it in a delusional *el* [being short for "elementalistic"] 'isolation' as the most important.

And further on:

... events are interconnected, that everything in this world influences everything else, and that happenings leave some traces everywhere.

So there is an interconnectedness, but there is also change. And change interested Korzybski a great deal. The use of dates, one of Korzybski's working devices, reminds us that we live in a process world, a world where everything is changing all the time—including us. Korzybski explicitly recognized this and said so.

In his Olivet Lectures, published in *General Semantics Seminar 1937*, he says at one point:

> I would deny that any electronic process is ever 'identical' with itself. Are you 'identical' with yourself from second to second? What you know about yourself should tell you that you are not 'identical' with yourself from moment to moment.

Sometimes Korzybski's examples may seem trivial. While it is technically true that you are not identical with yourself from second to second on some molecular level, that's not very interesting or significant; it's not how we experience the world.

But if you consider the idea a bit more, it can be really interesting and radical. The self is ever-changing, not only in terms of outward appearances or physical composition, but on the inside as well. One personal example on this front: I have kept a journal since 2005. One of the remarkable things you cannot help but learn in keeping a journal is how much you change.

When I read over earlier entries, I feel like I am reading the words of a completely different person with different interests and ideas. I feel like that because I *am* a different person. Perhaps my experience is more extreme than others, but I believe you would find much the same thing if you had kept a journal over the last two decades.

Even reading entries from just two years ago can be eye-opening. And the beauty of a journal is you cannot lie to yourself. You actually wrote those things, thought those thoughts. And now you do not think the same way. If you doubt what I say, start keeping a journal —write about what you think, and also note favorite books, authors, movies, music, foods, general thoughts on your life at that time, where you think are going, whatever. The changes you observe will astonish you.

On this idea of an ever-changing self: I want to share a passage from a book titled *A Study of Gurdjieff's Teaching* by Dr. Kenneth Walker, which was published in 1957.

One of the things Gurdjieff advocated was what he called *self-observation*, which is a way of looking at yourself almost as if you were another person, observing your doings, thoughts, and so forth. The idea of this exercise, if pursued diligently over a stretch of time, was that you would learn something important about yourself. And Walker certainly did.

He wrote, after a few months of diligent self-observation:

> I was surprised at the richness of the haul of observations I made during the next few days by observing myself... as though taking stock of some other person with whom I was only slightly acquainted.
>
> Perhaps the earliest and most disquieting of the findings made in this way was that I was never the same for more than few minutes, and yet I had the effrontery to preface many of my remarks with such misleading phrases as I always think that...' or 'I am convinced that...' or 'I feel strongly that...' What nonsense!

And who was it that was making this dogmatic statement about his own thoughts and his feelings? Who, in short, was 'I'?

Over two thousand years ago Heraclitus proclaimed that 'everything flowed,' and up till that moment I had imagined that in uttering these well-known words he was referring only to the world outside ourselves.

Now, as the result of only three month's self-observation, I realized that what was undoubtedly true of the world outside myself was equally true of the world within me. Everything flowed within me as it flowed without...

This wonderful passage is what got me thinking about this topic of a changing self again. So, what is the self exactly then? Is it a fictitious entity? A delusion?

On this point, I want to bring in another sage: Nisargadatta Maharaj (1897–1983), who was a famous guru in India. (Again, I am being extremely reductive here but...) He would have made a brilliant general semanticist. He emphasized the kind of holistic thinking I am writing about. In one talk, published in

I Am That: Talks with Sri Nisargadatta Maharaj (the source of all the Maharaj quotes which follow), he used the example of an electric lamp.

> It is because the lamp, the wiring, the switch, the transformer, the transmission lines and the power house form a single whole that you get the light. Any one factor is missing and there would be no light. You must not separate the inseparable. Words do not create facts; they either describe them or distort them. The fact is always non-verbal.

In that I see a lot of Korzybski. There is the idea of not separating the inseparable; Korzybski called separating the inseparable "elementalist" and keeping them together "non-elementalist" thinking. There is the idea that words are not the things they describe and that the beginning of experience is non-verbal—also very Korzybskian. And finally, 'the fact' is always non-verbal—which echoes Korzybski's notion of the unspeakable level.

As Maharaj says in another context:

> Be careful. The moment you start talking, you create a verbal universe: a universe of words, ideas, concepts and abstractions,

interwoven and interdependent, most wonderfully generating, supporting and explaining each other... yet, mere creations of the mind. Words create words; reality is silent.

Here is what Korzybski would call the unspeakable level of experience, which we can't reach with words but only "point our finger, insisting on silence." In this, Korzybski echoes a sentiment expressed by the ancient Greek philosopher Cratylus.

Cratylus was a follower of Heraclitus and took to its logical extreme the Heraclitian idea of everything being in flux. Aristotle tells us, in his *Metaphysics*, that Cratylus believed that it was better to say nothing, and so he would just point with his finger. Cratylus, Aristotle writes, "criticized Heraclitus for saying that one cannot enter the same river twice, for he himself held that it cannot be done even once." I don't take such an extreme position as Cratylus, though I am in great sympathy with him.

Back to Maharaj: Maharaj taught not to identify yourself with words and instead to be free of self-identification. "As long as you have all sorts of ideas about yourself, you know yourself through the mist of these ideas." He implored people to go beyond personal obsessions and unnecessary self-identification with its bundle of memories and habits and affiliations.

Instead he taught seeing yourself as not truly separate in order to cultivate a feeling of 'I am the world and the world is myself.' He said, "once it is established, there is just no way of being selfish... Everybody's welfare is one's own."

This sounds very similar to what Einstein told us. And consider the Korzybskian axiom: "Whatever you say a thing is, it isn't." Should this axiom not also apply to ourselves? We are not what we say, or perhaps we are not *only* what we say.

Maharaj also said, similar to Korzybski, "Whatever can be described cannot be yourself, and what you are cannot be described."

What Maharaj teaches is a form of detachment, with the aim of achieving an inner peace and tranquility, free from anxiety and fear. And a recognition that we are prolific creators of what are basically verbal prisons.

So then, how to answer the question posed at the start? Who are 'you'?

Maharaj once answered it this way: "I am nothing in particular, and yet I am." Or on another occasion, he said: "All I can say is 'I am'; all else is inference." This reminds me of Exodus 3:14. God said to Moses, "I AM WHO I AM."

These answers strike me as Korzybskian. Korzybski's ideas challenge basic, long-standing, assumptions. And what could be more basic than the notion of a separate self? Of a stable, identifiable 'I'?

I believe the idea of a stable, readily identifiable self is a sort of fiction—created by separating what is inseparable and by ignoring the wise insights I have been writing about.

But even if you don't buy my logic in its entirety, perhaps I can at least nudge you to take the idea of yourself and of your professed identities with more circumspection and more detachment.

Lastly, before we move on, a footnote to this talk of mine...

The previous evening I had dinner with a shaman from Los Angeles. Actually, he wasn't an actual shaman, but the CEO and founder of One Golden Thread, the talented and inimitable Jeff Scult.

I love One Golden Thread's clothes, and I wear them everyday when I can. Scult and I get along very well and think similarly about life, the universe, and everything. After dinner at the Soho House, he gave me a necklace—what he calls a 108 talisman. It's a handcrafted brass pendant that combines the number 108 into a distinctive image, which has become the logo of One Golden Thread.

The meaning of 108 is multi-layered, as Scult says on his website: "The sacred and mystical number 108 weaves through the universe, nature, science, non-dogmatic intention-based faiths, human body design, and modern day culture... and if you wish to see for yourself, google wiki 108." I'll leave that to you, but for now I want to highlight how Scult thinks about it: 1 is the self, 0 is the community, and 8 is the planet. And they all tie together, the unity of all things.

I told him, "You know, I'm about to give a presentation on this idea tomorrow." It's one of those weird synchronicities, one of those

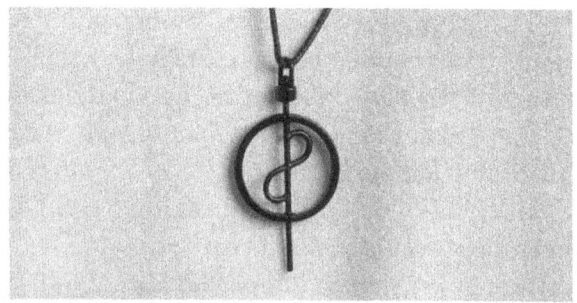

A 108 Talisman from One Golden Thread

times where the universe seems to be nudging you along, giving you some assurance that you are on the right path. At least, that's how I understood it.

Later, I shared my talk with Scult. Of course, he loved it. "Just read," he texted me. "Yes. Yes. Yes. As the infamous Dr. Bob said, 'Carry the message. And if you must, use words.'"

The Beedie Baba

Nisargadatta Maharaj is worth spending a little more time with. The old sage and Korzybski, odd as the pairing may sound, were not so far off on several points in their thinking. Before we get to that, let me introduce him a bit more.

Maharaj grew up in a poor family and had no formal education. I don't know much about his life, the details of which he would say are not important to know anyway. He lived in Mumbai and sold beedies, an Indian cigarette—hence his nickname, the "beedie baba." How he became a sought-after sage, I do not know either. Nonetheless, from his "humble tenement in the back lanes of Bombay" (in the words of his translator Maurice Frydman), Maharaj would hold court with visitors seeking his advice and wisdom. It was a small room, and his fame seemed modest in his lifetime, nothing compared with the crowds around the likes of Krishnamurti or Osho.

Maharaj espoused a simple philosophy, best illustrated by going through some choice exchanges with those who sought his wisdom. Maurice Frydman captured 101 of these talks in a volume titled *I Am That*, published in 1973.

I have read *I Am That* several times from cover to cover, plus there have been countless times where I have dipped into it and read passages here and there. As an aside, there are other collections of his talks. Yet as much as I love Maharaj's ideas, I've never picked up any of them. I don't know why. Perhaps because I cannot imagine how he can be any better than he is in *I Am That*. My copy is full of underlining and stars marking passages. I suspect the book has had a large influence on how I think about things.

Where to begin?

I think to begin I will say that Maharaj would fully endorse my verse:

> *Everything is connected*
> *to everything else.*
> *And everything is the way it is*
> *because <u>everything else</u> is*
> *the way <u>it</u> is.*

I know so, because my verse was largely inspired by reading his words. Thus, for Maharaj, there are no particular causes. As he says in talk 4, "the entire universe contributes to the existence of even the smallest thing; nothing could be as it is without the universe being what it is."

If you take this to heart and meditate deeply on the idea, you will find it changes how you think about everything. People and events take on a different color. Events that seem tragic will also seem necessary in an odd way. They had to happen that way. And if they didn't then everything else would also be different. Perhaps worse, perhaps better. It is impossible to know. But knowing that everything is one seamless movement makes one philosophical and less sure about what caused what.

The engine that drives 'events' is deeper and more opaque than most everyone assumes. Whenever I hear someone say, for example, "the Civil War was caused by X," I pause and think to myself, "the Civil War was caused by everything that went before it. Everything had to happen just as it happened." It doesn't mean we can't talk about it, but perhaps the kinds of questions we ask will change, and we will be more circumspect about our answers.

We ascribe wins and losses in sports to particular players, or economic prosperity (or contraction) to certain politicians, or successes (or failures) in life generally to the actions of individuals and so on and so on. But the causal links people like to talk about are way too narrow.

Causality was a topic Maharaj touched on often in his talks. Here he points to the fault of thinking in terms of causes:

> Once you create for yourself a world in time and space, governed by causality, you are bound to search for and find causes for everything. You put the question and impose an answer.

But what happens if you don't 'put' the question, in the same way I do not ask about free will and determinism, recognizing them as mere concepts? Stop looking for causes, and different thought-patterns will emerge.

For example, Majaraj's *everything* hypothesis, stated above, makes you think differently about people and challenges in your life. Suddenly that irritating neighbor or work colleague takes on a deeper purpose and meaning. They, too, had to be there just as they are. It could not happen any other way. Is it their fault? How can it be?

Events that seem disappointing at one stage of life deliver sweet fruit at another, and vice versa. Honors won seem doubtful later. Snubs turn into lucky misses. Victories turn into defeats, defeats turn into victories. Anyone who reflects on their life will find numerous times where the tables were turned, where things happened in unexpected ways, where events humbled us and humility walked in. Things happened. And keep on happening.

Things happen, as digestion or perspiration happens. "You do not need to worry about growing hair," Maharaj says in talk 7, "so I need not worry about words and actions. They just happen and leave me unconcerned, for in my world nothing ever goes wrong."

A hard teaching, as I like to say, but one that is liberating; and this is the core of Maharaj's philosophy, a path to achieve self-realization, or enlightenment, a feeling of perfect equanimity.

Often people are quick to jump on this and say, somehow, that equanimity means one should just do nothing, to not even try to make things 'better,' to give up. But not really. Maharaj, when confronted with such an objection, would say you can, and perhaps must, still dive into life with gusto. As he said in Talk 16, "work with enormous zeal, yet remain inwardly free," like a mirror that reflects but is otherwise unaffected itself. It is hard to live this way all the time, I have found, but even adding a bit of it to your life, like a potent spice, goes a long way.

Some people might say thinking in this way somehow limits your willingness to feel compassion or love. On the contrary, your compassion and love will grow because you will see everything as connected, and you will see yourself in all things. When I see a person, I imagine a long tail of history behind them that made them who they are—and made me who I am. We are all leaves on the same tree of life.

When I see a man who is down and out, I often think if I had started life where he did, I would be him. And if he started with my advantages, he'd be me. I appreciate him more and I feel for him. I will be patient and kind to him. I will see him as a human being. I will see that I could be him. More than that, I see that he *is* me. Or more specifically, he is *also* me. We are connected as one—no woo-woo or mysticism required.

The idea is to go ahead and live fully, but do not allow abstractions to bind you and cause you to suffer. See through them. Recast them, as Maharaj suggests. See it all as part of the whole, as the effect of everything that is.

Another element in Maharaj's thinking is to push back against our tendency to describe and label. He encourages us to try to see things as they are (remember the unspeakable level) and not as we imagine them with our words and descriptions. In an oft-used metaphor, Maharaj says if you take away the name and shape from jewelry, the gold becomes obvious. Maharaj wants us to see the gold, not be blinded by the name and form of events and patterns and things.

More importantly, these names and forms (abstractions as we've been calling them) impose on us in various ways. "Be free of name and form and of the desires and fears they create," he urges us.

This runs so against the thrust of the times we live in, where 'identity' is such a power in the world. Everyone seems so eager to take on a label—be it part of a religious or political or social movement, or a profession or a fan base or, gosh, the list goes on and on. Maharaj would have us drop it all and say no more than "I am."

As he says at the end of talk 13:

Consistently and perseveringly separate the 'I am' from 'this' or 'that' and try to feel what it means to *be*, to just *be*, without being 'this' or 'that.' All our habits go against it and the task of fighting them is long and hard sometimes...

This is easier to achieve. I do it all the time. I resist the urge to label myself as anything at all. And the effect is wondrous. No longer bound, I feel like I see things more as they are without being part of a 'team.' There is no 'rooting interest.' No longer bound, I change my mind freely, accept contradictions and paradoxes, and am at ease with varying viewpoints.

I have had discussions with friends about some of these ideas. The responses are always interesting. Some people, I think, like their chains. They enjoy being bound. They like the 'us' against 'them.' They like to divide and label. I don't know. It is an odd thing to me. But, as I've been saying, everything is—well, you can finish the rest!

Maharaj frequently wielded something close to Korzybski's Razor, as in this exchange:

Q: When I see something pleasant, I want it. Who exactly wants it?

M: The question is wrongly put. There is no 'who'. There is desire, fear, anger, and the mind says—this is me, this is mine. There is no thing which could be called 'me' or 'mine'. Desire is a state of the mind, perceived and named by the mind.

Here he calls into question the 'who.' There is no 'who.' There are only feelings that we call such and such, and this and that. See them as such and you will deal with them differently, with detachment.

Maharaj was also keenly aware of our polarities and the need to go beyond them. "When life and death are seen as essential to each other," he says in talk 12, "as two aspects of one being, *that* is immortality. To see the end in the beginning and the beginning in the end is the intimation of eternity."

I could provide many examples:

To know itself, the self must be faceted with its opposite—the non-self.

Movement and rest are states of mind and cannot be without their opposites.

Things and people are different, but they are not separate. Nature is one, reality is one. There are opposites, but no opposition.

It is true that all manifestation is in the opposites. Pleasure and pain, good and bad, high and low, progress and regress, rest and strife; they all come and go together.

After all, even universality and eternity are mere concepts, the opposites of being place and timebound. Reality is not a concept, nor the manifestation of a concept. It has nothing to do with concepts.

These provide a good summary of how he thinks on such topics, always remembering how everything is *connected*. His philosophy seems to cry out continuously, asking, "How do you know?" And he urges us to speak from our own experience.

He would often call out questioners who wanted to know if one theory was better than another. To him all theories were "ways of putting words together." That has the effect of quickly knocking them off their pedestals, letting us have a better look at them in the dirt. Ours is a world of mental images and words; let us not treat these too preciously.

One of my favorite exchanges is when a seeker seems exasperated with Maharaj's continued dismissal of the seeker's various abstractions—'righteousness,' 'god,' 'devotion' and so on. And the seeker finally says, "So all my questions, my search and study are of no use?" And Maharaj answers, "These are but the stirrings of a man who is tired of sleeping."

Maharaj is one our great sages and teachers. He epitomizes a way of thinking I am trying to portray in this book using Korzybski's tools. Granted, I am stretching Korzybski's ideas to extremes, but I think it is a project worth pursuing.

Note on Diogenes

Jean-Manuel Roubineau's book, titled *The Dangerous Life and Ideas of Diogenes the Cynic*, is worth a stop in our journey—cynicism here referring to a school of philosophy, contemporaneous with Stoicism or Epicureanism. Cynics scorned attachment to material things and cultivated a cosmopolitan outlook, among other things. I think of Diogenes as an example of someone who entirely shed any particular identity or attachment to place of birth and replaced it with a sense of being at home anywhere.

Diogenes was one of the most famous of the Cynics. He allegedly was involved in some sort of money counterfeiting scheme for which he was exiled from his home town of

Sinope. To the Cynic's way of thinking, exile was symbolically significant, as they regarded attachment to the city of one's birth as a kind of self-imprisonment. Exile was "the ultimate experience of detachment, renunciation, separation from everything one holds dear. It was altogether natural then, that the lives of noble exiles should have been erected into models of exemplary behavior."

Two quips from Diogenes are relevant to our discussion here. To someone who said to him that the Sinopeans have condemned Diogenes to exile, he retorted, "yes, I have condemned them to stay where they are."

And when asked where he was from, he said "I am a citizen of the world." And he also said, "Let me consider the universe my home." Again, it's worth emphasizing how significant this statement was for him as it ran counter to the prevalent Greek idea that one was tied to one's homeland, and to be separated from it was some kind of tragic fate.

People are very eager to belong to a team—whether professional, political, religious, ethnic, or whatever. But if you shed these, what is left? Wise was the person who could slip the chains of verbal descriptions, self-imposed or otherwise.

On this, I give the final word to Paul Brunton, a seeker who spent time with Bhagavan in India and wrote a bestseller about his journey titled *A Search In Secret India*.

"To None and To All"

"People sometimes ask me to what religion I belong or to what school of yoga I adhere. If I answer them, which is not often, I tell them: "To none and to all!"

If such a paradox annoys them, I try to soften their wrath by adding that I am a student of philosophy. During my journeys to the heavenly realm of infinite eternal and absolute existence, I did not once discover any labels marked Christian, Hindu, Catholic, Protestant, Zen, Shin, Platonist, Hegelian, and so on, any more than I discovered labels marked Englishman, American, or Hottentot. All such ascriptions would contradict the very nature of the ascriptionless existence. All sectarian differences are merely intellectual ones. They have no place in that level which is deeper than intellectual function.

He who has tasted of the pure Spirit's own freedom will be unwilling to submit himself to the restrictions of cult and creed.

Therefore, I could not conscientiously affix a label to my own outlook or to the teaching about this existence which I have embraced. In my secret heart I separate myself from nobody, just as this teaching itself excludes no other in its perfect comprehension. Because I had to call it by some name as soon as I began to write about it, I called it philosophy because this is too wide and too general a name to become the property of any single sect. In doing so I merely returned to its ancient and noble meaning among the Greeks who, in the Eleusinian Mysteries, designated the spiritual truth learnt at initiation into them as "philosophy" and the initiate himself as "philosopher" or lover of wisdom.

Why this eagerness to separate ourselves from the rest of mankind and collect into a sect, to wear a new label that proclaims difference and division? The more we believe in the oneness of life, the less we ought to herd ourselves behind barriers."

CHAPTER FIVE

Interlude Part 2: The Shadow

We pick up with the second interlude, as my guide and I continue our way from the ruins. More dream journaling…

***

We walk on and eventually come to a shadowed, rocky ravine where a small stone hut with a thatched roof sits. A slender white plume of blue smoke lazily wafts out of the chimney…

He motions me to go on. "I will wait here," he says.

I walk closer to the doorway and walk in…

Inside, I see a robed and sandaled man, with tousled brown hair and scraggly beard tending a fire. There is a pot simmering over the fire.

"Greetings," he says without looking. "I've been expecting you."

"Forgive me," I say, "but who are you?"

"Why the obsession with names and naming things?"

I think for a minute... not sure what to say. He stands up, facing me with a smile.

"Well, why were you expecting me?" I say.

"Because, you have had thoughts of me swimming around in your mind. I knew I was bound to make an appearance. I have always been there... It's the yin and yang, the dark and the light, up and down, right and left–they all need each other. They are all part of the one."

Again, I am quiet.

He says, "To know these things intellectually is one thing. To live them is another. This is your challenge. You say these things, but in life's ups and downs, you act and think differently."

"No argument," I quickly admit. "There is a certain amount of 'hard wiring' to overcome, or perhaps just accept. Slap me in the face and I will get angry. Inflict pain and I will want it to go away. I am not there... in the state of the Buddha just yet."

"Why not? If you want to get to the next room and the door is closed, you know enough to open it."

"It doesn't seem so simple."

"Because you don't really want it," he says rather sharply. Unlike my wizardly guide, this fellow doesn't bring feelings of warmth and care. "You say you do, but you also love your attachments. Your fetters are pleasant. Yet they remain fetters all the same. You are afraid to open the door."

"I fear you might be right, but I don't want to admit it."

"You want to figure out a way to have it both ways. It cannot be done. Teachers who say otherwise are like dry canals. As Jesus said, the way brings grief also. It is the message no one wants to hear, and for which they will throw stones.

"What other men call 'evil' or 'bad' or 'unfortunate' is just as necessary as their opposites and just as unreal. Everything just 'is.' You must get beyond moral judgements or you will get nowhere. Swallow your human pride and see beyond your mortal self.

"You need the 'villains' to have your 'heroes.' But the truth lies beyond these concepts. See beyond them. See them as just words, just concepts, just human made ideas, unreal, illusory... The Universe just is...

"The sooner you learn this, the sooner you will be free."

I tell myself I know what he is saying. I've written about it. I read about it. I've thought about it. I know the arguments and I feel their truth. And yet...

Later, I dip into the *Ashtavakra Gita*. My oh my, how I would love to sit with the author of this jewel-filled text! Ashtavakra's words sting, for I know I am the fool he speaks of (p. 65):

> The moment a fool gives up concentration
>   and his other spiritual practice,
> He falls prey to fancies and desires.
>
> Even after hearing the truth,
>   The fool clings to his folly.
> He tries hard to look calm and composed,
>   But inside he is full of cravings.

Full of cravings. I can't sit for more than an hour without those cravings peeping in. I want this and I want that... I want to do this and I want to do that... wishing for this to happen and not that...liking this person and not liking that person...

Hard to just sit still and just be... not needing anything, not judging anybody or anything, just living in the present, content, come what may...

INTERLUDE PART 2: THE SHADOW

Ruminating on the unnamed man in the hut, I come to think he reflects the "darker" side of my personality, the side I don't want to admit is there, the side I overlook, the side I try to ignore, the side I find embarrassing, the side I have trouble overcoming, the side I wish to hide... He brings it out and forces me to look at it, acknowledge it, embrace it, get past shame, get past ego... This Shadow, as I call him, is an important healer, a truth teller, a potent pairing with the wise old man in the blue robe, who together present an integrated personality, a holy egg forged from all things...

I write of 'truth'—but again what is that? Another word, another human idea, another vapor, another spook?

Expressing what I feel in these pages is most difficult. I have great sympathy with those who practiced *via negativa*.

But back to the sandaled man with the tousled brown hair...

I ask the Shadow, somewhat irritated. "If I must accept all things, then, too, I accept my fetters. Why should I bother with this challenge you lay down?"

The shadow laughs and says, "Get to this state first and then see if those questions arise."

I feel a flash of anger: "Do you know what you are talking about? Or are you another would-be sage mumbling nonsense? Do you expect me to sit here in awe? I am not awed."

"Keep going. I am amused."

"Why struggle? It is in the nature of things to—"

"—struggle?"

"—it is the nature of things to be fettered and blinkered."

"Not for you."

"Why am I special?"

"You are not special. I never said you were." The Shadow turns back to his fire.

"Then why should I bother with this struggle…"

"Because it is in your nature to do so. You can't help it. Why are you here at all? If you're so sure that sitting there fettered and blinkered is no better or worse than to be free, then why are you here? Go ahead and go back to drinking the numbing potions of the world. The door is there. Goodbye to you, then."

I do not move. The Shadow chuckles, as if he had successfully called my bluff. He grabs his pot with a mitted hand and puts it on a small table set with two bowls. "What I serve, you are hesitant to take. You are afraid of it... So, sit or leave. It does not matter."

I sit. And my anger and annoyance drains aways. I feel calmer. "I know it doesn't matter. Whatever happens, happens. This much I understand. And therefore this... effort, struggle, whatever you want to call it... moves on its own accord, or by the powers that move all things."

"That is it," he says. "Frustration and anger will do you no good... but accept whatever comes, even frustration and anger. Seek to move beyond it."

"Life is a funny thing," I say. "I have no control, yet I must play the game as if I do."

We eat the stew that he has served and it is delicious beyond all words. When we are finished, I sense it is time for me to go.

"Thank you," I say, standing up. "I think it is time for me to go."

"Continue to think about what we have said here. You will see."

I bow and head out. I find my wise old guide sitting under a tree, further up the pass near where we entered the ravine. He stands up and motions for me to come. I walked up to him.

"Are you ready?" he says. "We have further to go, much further."

"I am." I hesitate, fumbling for the right words.

"No need to say anything," he says. "I know."

"Alright, then, let's go."

He leads the way, staff in hand, and I follow as we continue to walk our path...

Bare Feet on Dirt

[An interlude within an interlude. Another day, another dreamy vision, but this one is different...]

I am alone before an open green gate in my bare feet on dirt.

It is hot. I hear monkeys in the trees.

I walk through the open gate and head to a small hall. It is very hot and humid and I am already sweating.

I walk in the hall. The stone floor is cool to my feet, the temperature drops from being out of the sun. My eyes take several seconds to adjust.

I see an Indian man sitting on a couch. He wears nothing but a kaupina. He seems in deep thought.

I walk up to him... I know who he is! I have so many questions for him. I am filled with excitement to meet him. Just to see him is thrilling. Just to be in his presence feels like a miracle...

I drop to my knees. He looks at me. All questions evaporate. My mind is still. I can think of nothing to say. I am washed over with a deep sense of peace. Everything is perfect. Time is non-existent. My own sense of self melts into everything else. Pure awareness....

He looks at me. And that is all I remember.

The Library

Another day, another dream, another portal into the deeper self opens...

I stand in a huge, old, ornate library. The ceilings are incredibly high. The aisles are so long, I cannot see their end.

Human beings are the only creatures who read. It is an odd thing when you think about it. No other animal creates such things. Piles of words, symbols...

I live a life full of reading books, my eyes focused on symbols on a page. And pages and pages of symbols. Walls covered in books. Always reading books. Always getting books. I must have a thousand in my library. I must've given away ten times that over my lifetime. Maybe more. The library has turned over considerably over the years as my interests shift, as I grow and develop and learn—so I like to think. (Also I moved a couple of times, which always seems to force me into getting rid of stuff!)

The old wizard is beside me again, gazing on the many shelves of books. He says, almost in a whisper: "The result of much human toil—energy, attention, time, labor…"

"Yes. And I can't help but wonder was it worth it? I think it must've been—for the authors. To work out one's ideas and thoughts gives them a depth and maturity. They change and grow and invite new thoughts and ideas… So much wisdom, but at the cost, too—I must say it—of a lot of… I want to say 'drivel' or 'nonsense' but I know such a judgment would be to misread the nature of humankind's existence. And who is to say what is waste and drivel? And who can possibly know what the full ring of effects were, the knock-on effects, the tangential effects… Something seemingly insignificant can turn out to be the keystone of the entire arch, so to speak."

"You are learning," the old man says. "All of it is an essential part of a creative process. Nothing is wasted. Everything happened exactly as it must."

"I love books, as you know. I've been an avid reader all my life. What I have read has challenged me and changed me. Books have opened up worlds that I would never have discovered on my own. They have lent me the expertise, wisdom and experience of those who have lived before me. They have given me

an immeasurable amount of pleasure.
I cannot imagine a world without books."

The old man says, "They are humankind's special thing. Alone in the animal kingdom."

I reply, "The sages will say you cannot become self-realized by reading books. There are so many books. So many ideas. One is apt to get lost, follow dead trails, read for reading's sake. I don't know. I suppose there are pitfalls. But I have found incredible treasures, invaluable pointers."

"The sages' warning on book reading is to guard against laziness," the old man says. "It is too easy to read a book—full of the digested thoughts of another—and simply repeat them, to know them intellectually, but not work it out yourself, not really understand it... The analogy is old, but good—to rely too much on books is a bit like having someone else chew your food... You need to chew your own food. By all means, absorb what wisdom you can glean from those who came before you, but be sure to work with it, knead it with your own experiences. Mix, mix and mix again... That is the great reward of a human life of the mind."

"That is a very appealing vision, old wizard. However, the life of the mind is not for everyone. Some do not read at all."

"And that is as it should be, as it must be. It cannot be any other way. Work out your own destiny, and worry not about the destiny of others. You have plenty of work to do on yourself."

"I can do nothing else, so it would seem. But I feel I can choose different paths."

"You can and you do. Nonetheless, everything happens as it must."

"That doesn't make sense," I say.

"It is a paradox. You think and you choose—so it seems to you. But there is a script nonetheless and you are akin to an actor in a play—who seems to struggle and think and choose… but the script unfolds in any case."

"How can one know this? You can't prove it."

"I don't need to prove anything."

"Who writes the script?"

He laughs, that warm merry laugh. "Don't be so literal."

"You frustrate me. You seem to know the answers, but you speak in riddles. Maybe you're full of you-know-what," I say it jokingly.

"Maybe I am. How would you know?"

"I can think through what you are saying. Of course, you will say it doesn't matter. Maybe it doesn't. I must behave as if I can choose. There is no other way for me to be."

"I agree."

"So what is the point of repeating, 'everything happens as it must' or whatever variation of the same?"

"Must there be a point? What is the point of all these books? What is the point of anything anybody ever does?"

"There you go again! Don't answer my questions with more questions. Answer my question. Why tell me 'everything happens as it must' if it makes no difference in how I behave?"

His eyes widened. "But it does make a difference. You are more aware. You are more attune to the grand universe, the nature of existence and being, if you accept this view of everything you see and think as being part of what happens in a movie…"

"I have heard wise sages use this analogy. Our life is like the images on a screen. They come and they go. The screen itself, however, remains unaffected by all that happens."

"That is it. Be the screen."

I laugh. "Be the screen?"

"You are already the screen. You just don't realize it, fully, yet."

"But how can I live that way? I choose, but I don't choose… I suppose it takes the pressure off existence. I can't do anything other than what I do."

"Get to that state first, then see if you still have the question." He smiles.

"You say people have to work things out for themselves… that makes no sense in the context of everything happening as it must. They have no choice but to work it out, as is their destiny."

"Exactly right."

"Then why admonish people to not be lazy in reading books!"

"Think of the script," he says. "The movie. We are actors. We must play the role. I am playing the role. You are playing the role. Even your resistance and questioning is part of the script."

What he says seems… hard to believe.

If he is right, then we are parts of a whole… bits of consciousness and awareness… thoughts flowing through us, ideas digested, mixed, actions performed, 'choices' made… but all of it part of the grand system. Nothing out of place. Nothing other than what it must be.

So, to understand that, deeply, in one's bones, in the soul, means… what?

Well, it would seem to mean a change in how we look at the world. We'd see it with greater acceptance and equanimity, especially when dealing with events that seem unfavorable, with people you don't like, with anything that seems to get in your way...

Envy dissolves. Hate dissolves. Sorrow blows away. Anxiety withers. Instead a kind of peacefulness grows. Patience. Tolerance. Even love. It does not mean a passionless, dull life. It does not mean one must give up on the world or not try. It does mean all such pursuits occur with greater awareness and inner detachment.

After a time, I say, "I am seeing, now, more the truth of what you say... It is still hard to believe there is a script. But it does not seem unreasonable. The rest of the natural world seems to operate thus. The movement of stars and planets. The weather. The oceans... Why would humanity then be the exception? Or does the Sun choose its path each day? Does wind decide when to blow? Perhaps the earth has a soul, as Jung said."

"There is no harm in looking at the world that way."

"As organic, conscious? As choosing?"

He nodded. "It amounts to the same thing in the end."

"Does it?"

"Most of humanity behaved this way for thousands of years. 'All things are full of gods,' is the old wisdom of the Platonic tradition. And so offerings to their gods, praying, etc. What is all that, except to influence the choosing?"

"But how is it the same thing as 'the world happening as it must?'" I ask.

"Because prayers seemingly are answered or they are not. Whatever happens, people must accept it. And as they accept it, they will come to the same end and realize they play a role."

"Maybe so, but they will act differently, it seems to me. I am thinking of all the religious zealots who think their view is the divinely inspired view and everybody else is wrong. That is a view that does not inspire tolerance. On the contrary, it seems to fuel hate."

"In some, yes. But again... there is a role for all of that. There is no movie without villains. Diversity moves the plot. Maybe you can't see the end or purpose or meaning behind any of it. But that does not mean they are not there. Think again of the system view, the organic whole. Everything is needed. Everything is connected to everything else and contributes, in some way, to everything else—not only now, but forevermore... and in fact, what exists now is built on everything that happened before."

I sigh. "I have long held a prejudice against the dogmatism of religion."

"Part of the role you must play. But you can play the role—now—with more circumspection. You can live ironically."

I say to the old wizard, "There are certain tough questions in life that never seem to have answers. How many smart and wise minds have toiled over questions like "Do we have free will?" "What is consciousness? "Does God exist?" They never go away. And we never seem to get anywhere in answering them.

"When I come across such a question—one that has been asked for millennia—I think there must be something wrong with the question. Maybe wrong is not the right word. But something about the question that makes it inherently uncrackable. Most of the time, I find, it is because they embed certain human concepts—made up ideas. We can use language to create all kinds of questions that make no sense. For example, "How much does the color blue weigh?" This is a perfectly grammatically correct question... but conceptually it is, shall we say, problematic... The problem is we can devise other questions where it is not so clear that they are conceptually problematic.

"So, 'do we have free will?' sounds okay... but is it a problematic question like asking 'how much does the color blue weigh'? As Spinoza put it—"

And there I stop myself because I see, sitting there on the bookshelf, a copy of his *Ethics*.

The old man says, "Ah, Spinoza..."

I pull out the *Ethics* and read where Spinoza says a "decision of mind which is believed to be free is not distinguished [or perhaps "not distinguishable"] from imagination itself." He goes on to say those who "believe that they do anything from a free decision of the mind, dream with open eyes."

I snap the book closed and put it back. "Spinoza was indeed wise. And by all accounts, he seemed an affable and contented fellow. Honest, obliging, peaceful... he lived frugally. The answers he found, it seems, were good enough for him. He lived them and found satisfaction, even self-enlightenment perhaps... It is easy to love Spinoza for these things."

"He found his way," the old man nodded. "Everyone must work out their own way. You cannot live the way of another."

"No," I say. "But I can learn from them."

"Most certainly," he agrees.

I continue my little monologue: "There is another idea here that is important... and that is the idea of surpassing, or transcending, these human concepts—such as good and evil, freedom and slavery, right and wrong... These are ideas; they do not exist out there, in our experience. To say something is 'good' is to make a judgment. And the judgments can get in the way of seeing... they form part of the fog that obscures that screen we were talking about. They are part of the illusions to pierce... But this is hard to make people understand."

"Don't worry about other people," he says gently. "Find out who you are first."

Cliffs Overlooking the Sea

I had thought deeply about his advice. Next time I saw him, we stood on cliffs overlooking the sea. There was nothing but rock and water and sky, the soft cry of birds, the song of the sea and a salty breeze. The sun was low in the sky, making its way toward the horizon.

"Old man, there is a problem with your advice."

"And what is that?"

"I have thought long and hard about this 'finding out who I am.' How is one to disentangle what is authentically one's own and what is the world's? How am I to know what ideas I have are really my own and not merely absorbed from other people of my time and place in history? Even the language I speak is one I have been given. It divides the world into bits and pieces and I inherit the jigsaw puzzle...

"My answer to these questions is that the idea of an authentic self is just another idea, another concept. There is no such thing."

He says: "Do you not have experiences that only you have had? That have only been seen through your eyes? Felt through your body? No one has lived the life you have lived, as you have experienced it. Does that not give you the raw material of an authentic self?"

"Such an 'authentic self' is temporal and contingent. It is not much more than... a wave of the sea."

The old man responds, "If everything is connected to everything else, then those connections form an eternal and timeless bond. That is the self, your self.... You are part of everything, a happening, a wave in the ocean... but also for a time a unique manifestation of the universe—like a leaf on a tree, a snowflake falling from the sky... at once part of everything, but also, for a time, something unique.

Understanding this is what it means to know the self, to see this bigger picture and not lose hold of it in living your life."

I reply, "When you first introduced yourself to me, you said you were the 'one who knows himself.' Is this what you meant? That you understood this self?"

"Yes."

The old fellow continues, "You know something that nobody knows. If you put some attention toward yourself, you will discover things that only you will ever know. You will know yourself... Only you can do this, no one else can do it for you..."

CHAPTER SIX

The World 'Out There'

Out of the dream world and back to our world; or maybe out of one dream world and back into another. In this chapter, we look more closely at our descriptions and what we can say about the world 'out there.' The challenge is old. As Plato expressed through Euthyphro in the dialogue of the same name: "But Socrates, I do not know how to tell you what I mean. Somehow everything I propose goes round in circles on us and will not stand still."

***

At this point in our journey, we've come to understand there is a 'world out there,' for lack of a better term. And then there are our abstractions drawn from that ocean of possible experience.

Ergo, any search for 'truth' as something to be found or discovered seems lost at the start. As philosopher Richard Rorty (1913-2007) wrote in his book *Contingency, Irony, and Solidarity:*

The truth cannot be out there—cannot exist independently of the human mind—because sentences cannot so exist, or be out there. The world is out there, but descriptions of the world are not.

I read Rorty as saying something similar to Korzybski's "whatever we say a thing is, it isn't." The "world out there," sans our descriptions, is Korzybski's unspeakable level.

I am not aware that Rorty ever read Korzybski or knew anything about general semantics. There seems to have been minimal engagement between the general semantics camp and Rorty—at least if the archives of *ETC* (the Institute's flagship publication) and *General Semantics Bulletin* are any indication. A search for Rorty's name yields only a handful of mentions in total—a couple of footnotes, a couple of quotes, but nothing of substance. But I see quite a bit of overlap in their respective projects.

Rorty described himself as a pragmatist, and his favorite philosopher was John Dewey. Rorty's brand of pragmatism has many affinities with Korzybski's general semantics; chief among them would be his mindfulness of abstractions and a focus on how such abstractions hang together in relationships with other abstractions.

But first let us look at this idea of the "truth cannot be out there." I wrote about this idea in my book, *Dear Fellow Time-Binder: Letters on General Semantics*. I would like to borrow a bit from that book in this next section.

"The World Does Not Speak"

"The world does not speak," Rorty wrote, "only we do." Descriptions of the world, crafted by human nervous systems, can be judged and compared against other descriptions by human nervous systems. Over time, we replace older descriptions (the earth is flat) with newer descriptions (the earth is round) that we think are 'better.' And 'better' means more useful (i.e., it allows us to do more things, to talk about more things, explain more events, make better predictions, etc.)

Ergo, there is no objective world out there, no final arbiter of descriptions where we say, "Ah, that's it, we have it pinned down now." We can never have it pinned down. We can always replace one description with another description, one that seems better for our needs at hand.

Moreover, it is not always easy to know which description is 'better.' What passes for 'best description' today can be bettered tomorrow, just as Einstein 'improved' on Newton, and as quantum mechanics 'bettered' Einsteinian physics in some respects. It doesn't mean the old way was 'wrong' or 'untrue'—it simply means a more useful description, as we've been discussing, has emerged.

In the social realm of politics, practical living, religion, etc., there is a profusion of descriptions. Which description of the world is 'better'—the one offered by this party or that party? Which description is better, the one offered by the Stoics or the Epicureans? Which description is better, the one offered by Christians or Hindus? (Even within these categories, of course, there is debate—i.e., descriptions of $Christian_1$ may be very different on the same topics as $Christian_2$, or even $Christian_{1525}$ versus $Christian_{2025}$, etc.)

The point here is that there is no "final vocabulary," as Rorty put it. I think even writers on general semantics can sometimes give the impression that the territory is an objective thing against which we can check our maps.

For example, we know the map is not the territory... but the territory is not something we can know in all its ever-changing details. We're always making inferences based on what we can detect. Knowing this should both keep us humble with regard to our currently held descriptions (both those borrowed, or learned from, others and those we make for ourselves from our own experiences) and more open-minded about the descriptions of others.

Thanks to Rorty's *Philosophy as Poetry* (which I will talk about more in a minute), I now imagine, even when reading the works of philosophers and other thinkers, that I am reading the works of poets. A philosopher, such as Spinoza or Schopenhauer, is a poet of a kind. Philosophers offer a way to see the world. But for us, there should be no pressure to decide who was 'right.' We can enjoy what they offer in the same spirit we would enjoy Robert Frost or Emily Dickinson.

In this view, new theories and ideas are not representations of the 'real world,' not maps of an objective territory, but they are "poetic achievements," to use Rorty's phrase. The question of which set of maps is 'right' need not arise. "The answer to a great poem is a still better poem," Rorty wrote.

Our imaginations, our ability to interpret and create, propel us to write more poems, to make progress is the sort of progress embedded in the concept of time-binding. The result is a richer treasury of descriptions from which to choose and more recipes to follow and tinker with, all unburdened by the notion that there is a "final answer" at which such progress must stop.

'Things' As 'Numbers'

Okay, that is where I stopped with *Dear Fellow Time Binder*. But since I wrote that book, these ideas have percolated in my mind, and I want to elaborate a bit more here.

First, I should point out that Rorty is not saying even his own philosophy better corresponds to 'the world out there.' Instead, Rorty is trying to get away from the idea of correspondence itself, to get away from the idea that the world itself has some intrinsic nature. In fact, he advises not using the phrase "intrinsic nature" at all, since it is "more trouble than it has been worth."

Let me give a tangible example of what it means to think this way.

I said earlier that one of the affinities Rorty has with general semantics is an emphasis on understanding 'things' in terms of relationships with other 'things.' This is much in line with Korzybski.

As Korzybski wrote, "there is no such thing as an object in absolute isolation." Everything is related to everything else. Korzybski teaches us to think of any organism as a whole, embedded in an environment. These teachings help us see the world around us as ever-changing and interconnected. Following from this is another idea about the inadequacy of labels to capture it all. Korzybski advised us to abandon the 'is' of identity. All of these ideas prevent us from falling into dogmatic assertions about definitions, about what things 'really' are.

Rorty, too, emphasizes this point. His book *Pragmatism as Anti-Authoritarianism* includes an essay titled "Pan-Relationalism." There he pushes against the idea of "word pictures" and instead seeks to replace that idea with a "picture of a flux of continually changing relations, relations whose terms are themselves dissoluble into a nexus of further relations." In language reminiscent of Korzybski, he sets this position against the essentialism of Aristotle.

And here we get to something like a Korzybskian extensional device. You may recall Korzybski's extensional devices, which I have been using in this book: the single quotation mark, the date, etc. and the index.

Rorty suggests thinking of things as numbers. "The nice thing about numbers, for my present purpose," he writes, "is just that it is very difficult to think of them as having intrinsic natures."

So, let us take the number 10. What can we say about the number 10? We can say it is more than 5, but less than 15. We can say it is the sum of 7 and 3. We can describe it as the difference between 12 and 2. We can say lots of things about the number 10, but all these descriptions only relate 10 to other numbers. They say nothing about any intrinsic nature of the number 10.

Moreover, there would be no point or profit in trying to defend the position that 10 has an intrinsic definition, or an absolute nature. As Rorty says, "It doesn't pay to be an essentialist about numbers." (Empedocles, using the razor, said "Nothing that is has a nature. But only mixing and parting of the mixed, and nature is but a name given them by men"—as quoted by Aristotle in his *Metaphysics*.)

And in that same way, it doesn't pay to be an essentialist about "tables, stars, electrons, human beings, academic disciplines, social institutions, or anything else." Instead, think of 'things' as embedded in a web of relations. There is nothing to know about 'things' except an infinitely large number of descriptions about these relations.

Thus, whenever you have a term, or phrase, or concept whose meaning you are puzzling over, you might think of it as a number. Perhaps, in the spirit of Korzybski we could even add a "#" after whatever we are trying to define, as in "American#" or "general semantics#" to remind us to think in terms of relationships and usefulness instead of trying to arrive at a static essentialist definition.

Thinking this way has some positive effects. It gets you away from the idea of seeking some permanent, unvarying 'truth'—about anything. Instead you focus on practical matters, such as asking if a new description may be more useful to the task at hand than an older description. You allow yourself to be open to potential better descriptions, since you are not anchored in the mud of some 'truth.' No description is held to be 'closer to the truth' than any other; all descriptions do is give you different ways of talking about 'things' or ideas. In the same way, saying 10 is the sum of 7+3 is no more 'true' than saying 10 is more than 5 but less than 15. They are simply different ways of talking about the number 10.

The answer to any question about what a certain word or concept means, then, is a story about how people use them and how they relate to other words and concepts. These uses and relationships can change, depending on purposes to which they are put. They are contingent on time and place.

Philosophy as Poetry

In *Philosophy as Poetry*, which grew out of a series of lectures, Rorty writes about how there is a reluctance to embrace these ideas in part because of "the fear that imagination goes all the way down—that there is nothing to talk about that we might not talk about differently." And this fear causes people to posit some form of ultimate reality, some kind of bedrock truth. For Rorty, our descriptions are only limited by our imagination.

This is not to denigrate our descriptions. For example, the phrase "inalienable human rights" does not say anything about the nature of human beings. It isn't that "inalienable human rights" are close to some unchanging 'reality.' They are "noises and marks," but they lead to better social practices—better in the sense of more people living richer lives than ideas which treat human beings as property.

This reminds me of what Neil Postman once wrote about the term "sanitation engineer" as a replacement for "garbage man." The person who wants to make this change does not do it because "sanitation engineer" somehow more accurately reflects the intrinsic nature of the job. The change simply reflects a hope that the person doing this task might be treated with more respect and dignity than otherwise. If it works, the change is a 'better' social practice in a Rortian sense.

It also reminds me of many present day political debates—debates about what we call people, what pronouns we use, what gender people claim. These are debates between people who want to preserve one set of descriptions against a newer set of redescriptions.

Language, too, plays a role in wars and territorial disputes, which involve descriptions and what claims follow from these descriptions. Before the bullets fly, there is a battle over words.

During the pandemic of 2020, we saw one consequence of thinking 'science' can give us some final 'truth' about the virus or masks or vaccines. Because of this thinking, people saw any change in scientific opinions regarding these things as evidence of bad faith or of some conspiracy.

Instead, a view in line with Rorty and Korzybski would see scientific knowledge as descriptions subject to reinterpretation and change. Under such a view, change is normal, even expected. One would no more expect a final answer from a scientist than one would expect a poet to write a final poem from which no one would have any reason to attempt to write another, different poem.

To sum up, as Rorty says, "we shall never find descriptions so perfect that imaginative redescription will become pointless. There is no destined terminus to inquiry."

In this view, the arc of human thought isn't pulled magnetically to anything called 'truth,' nor does it spiral toward a better approximation of something called 'reality.' Instead, human thought is a creative act, a search for better descriptions, or, at least, "socially useful novelties," in Rorty's phrase.

What's Out There Then?

Korzybski may not have gone as far as Rorty regarding the idea that there are

THE WORLD OUT 'THERE'

no "things as they really are." After all, Korzybski's idea of "similar in structure" seems to imply an objective empirical world that we can get to know, against which we can check our descriptions. (Although, I think steady use of what I'm calling Korzybski's Razor takes you where Rorty is.) Whereas Rorty's main emphasis in checking our descriptions involves testing for some aspect of usefulness. Rorty says we "go astray when [we] succumb to the yearning for grandeur and start claiming to have discovered things as they really are."

Rorty does not think that there is a 'reality' out there for us to get right because there are no norms for talking about it. In other words, we call our beliefs true when we have rational justification from other people... but "other people" just means people who play the same language game as we do.

Rorty presents his ideas in a far richer way than I can here and defends them against an array of possible objections. All I want to establish is that these ideas echo Korzybskian themes and supplement the Razor. I hope to have demonstrated that similarity and perhaps persuade you to recognize the value in Rorty's formulations. (If you are interested in reading more by Rorty, a good entry point would be *Philosophy as Poetry*, followed by *Contingency, Irony and Solidarity*.)

What's out there, then? I'd say 'What's out there' is limited only by our imagination and our ability to create new ways of thinking "whose adoption may or may not be a good thing," as Rorty put it. I am reminded, too, of *Martin Heidegger: Basic Writings*, which starts with a lovely passage in the foreword:

> In his lecture course on Nietzsche in 1936, Heidegger said, "All great thinkers think the same. Yet this 'same' is so essential and so rich that no single thinker exhausts it."

Truth and The Universal Liability

I am not suggesting we casually throw out the idea of 'truth.' What I am advocating is we should take great care with any notions of truth we cast with our words. We ought to respect what cannot be spoken of, except with great difficulty. When it comes to 'truth,' I don't see how we escape what William James called the "universal liability" in *The Varieties of Religious Experience*:

> Since it is impossible to deny secular alterations in our sentiments and needs, it would be absurd to affirm that one's

own age of the world can be beyond correction by the next age. Skepticism cannot, therefore, be ruled out by any set of thinkers as a possibility against which their conclusions are secure; and no empiricist ought to claim exemption from this *universal liability*. [emphasis added]

James doesn't exempt religion from this liability either. James writes about the changes humans make to their religions over time; beliefs change, gods change. Our gods reflect our needs and views. When a god/religion no longer serves a purpose, we change it or supplant it.

Skepticism and doubt are something you can never fully escape.

Ironically, if you start with doubt, you eventually end up in the realm of the religious, of speculation and of belief. Because you inevitably start to doubt even your 'reason'; you see 'intuition' and 'experience' as at least its equal and perhaps its better. Or even better, you see them as distinctions without a difference.

You start to realize the boundaries between, say, 'science' and 'religion,' or 'truth' and 'fiction', or 'true' and 'false', all dissolve... There is only one thing, which I hesitate to name.

And it is in this realm that transcends human concepts, goes beyond the world of opposites. In this realm, you find yourself in the company of mystics, prophets, seers, magicians...

Peter Kingsley, in his book *Reality*, appreciates this irony as well. In writing about Parmenides and his idea that all thought ought to be treated as 'real', Kingsley writes:

> The irony is that by accepting every thought he is actually taking us beyond thought: showing us it doesn't matter, helping us to leave it all behind.

This line of thought shuts down thinking and distinctions such as 'true' and 'false,' 'good' and 'bad.' And here I love Kingsley's analogy of colors:

> It's like watching hundreds of colors, each of them trying to persuade you it happens to be the most important one—and then stepping back and seeing they all form a single rainbow...

Beautiful imagery. All of our abstractions form a single rainbow. "Everything is one," as Kingsley says, "And this end to discrimination is the end of all wisdom, the end of philosophy—and its beginning."

These thoughts echo those of Carl Jung. Over the years, reading Jung changed my view on religions generally and how to think about various myths or stories. For example, it no longer mattered whether Jesus Christ was 'really' resurrected or not. What mattered was what this story means; what wisdom does his teachings hold? What reaction do you have to it? How do people interpret the resurrection and what does it say about them? There are, in other words, many more interesting questions to think about. To obsess over whether it 'actually happened' is to miss the point of human storytelling entirely. And potentially closes you off to the rich inventory of wisdom embedded in these stories.

In a similar manner, I remember reading the tenth conversation in *Lament of the Dead*, a record of a conversation between Sonu Shamdasani and James Hillman about Jung's *Red Book*. They talk about the idea of "folk psychology," which Shamdasani describes as "nonprofessional forms of self-understanding that give rise to different forms of human self-consciousness." And here he makes what I thought at the time was a rather astonishing admission: "It doesn't matter if they are true or not, these themselves are remarkable inventions, remarkable creations. They've taken great ingenuity."

Shades of Rorty's philosophy as poetry. Later Shamdasani describes folk psychology again as a way people explain themselves and others. Simple. 'Truth' never enters into it. They are paths people take.

I like the word *path* here as a way to describe people's folk psychologies, religions, beliefs, philosophies. A path is not a process, not a dogma. Paths wander. Paths change as you go along. Paths involve choices. And there is more than one path. Paths may also differ in difficulty. Paths also involve mystery; you don't necessarily know where they will go, where they may take you. There is an element of surprise.

Which brings us to an age-old question.

Free Will vs. Determinism

> "We blame everyone and everything in sight for bad experiences—including ourselves—whereas we are simply out of our depth in cosmic learning. Blaming yourself sounds like humility but it is (more likely) conceit. What makes us so proud as to think that we could have stopped at all, even if we started it all?

> We haven't understood anything and least of all ourselves, and our own roles in the cosmos."

—Stafford Beer, *Think Before You Think*

Do we have free will? Or is everything already determined? Or something in between?

One side will say: Of course, I choose. I can have tea or coffee. I can go to the gym or stay home. I can have pizza for dinner or I can have pancakes if I want. I choose. It is obvious.

The other side might say, well do you? Perhaps your choices were already baked in the cake. Your choice was an illusion. Fate rules the world. Fate is not something to believe in or not. Fate is there. It is what pushes, pulls, happens. Fate is something you accept or else you wail in vain protest. You had no say in where or when you were born. Your genetic makeup, the language you speak, the hardwiring you readily acknowledge, and so on and so on. It is obvious you don't choose.

Or you might pick one of the gray areas in between. Some things you choose, but other things you can't. I don't think any of these arguments hold up for the simple reason that eventually, somewhere, a choice is going to butt up against the determined path. Which prevails? If free will prevails then clearly determinism is false. If determinism prevails, then choices made will be exposed as obvious illusions; they never mattered. They are conflicting realities.

Or you might argue that for all intents and purposes it seems you choose. It may well be an illusion, but it is a super powerful illusion, and you must live it. You must act as if you choose, because (ironically) you don't have a choice.

Or you can wield the Razor. 'Free will' and 'determinism' are words made up by human beings. There is no such thing as 'free will.' There is no such thing as 'determinism.' What are we arguing about? Phantoms of the mind. The arrangement of words in one way versus the arrangement of words in another.

Recasting the question this way brings the question down to a livable level, to where the soles of our shoes touch the sidewalk, where we hear traffic noise, breathe in the smell of the halal hawker and try to avoid walking into the people around us on the street.

"Oh, but you've just dismissed the question," you say. "You've just brushed aside an important question as a word game."

I have, because it is. And it is not an 'important' question. One of our sages,

THE WORLD OUT 'THERE'

Nisargadatta Maharaj, said it better than I can. In *I Am That*, talk 61, he's asked about free will and destiny. Maharaj says:

> You can have it as you like it. You can distinguish a pattern in your life or see merely a chain of accidents. Explanations are meant to please the mind. They need not be true. Reality is undefinable and indescribable.

You can say whatever you want. But in the end, it doesn't amount to much more than an aesthetic. You can read those philosophy books if you'd like. After all, we have to do something with the time that is given to us. Why not read books and ponder big questions like this?

All the explanations, as Maharaj rightly says, please the mind. They don't change the world you actually live in. I hesitate to call it 'reality' because what is *that*? Unless by 'reality' we mean the world we live in. The world we live in is the world of sand and waves and sun and wind—or, less glamorously, the world of grocery checkout lanes and parking spaces, of tax forms and bank accounts. What is 'free will' and 'determinism' worth in these settings?

Korzybski's Razor, if nothing else, clarifies the question. It leads you to a line of questioning within the question. It prompts you to ask "what is the wisdom in trying to answer this question?" or "does it matter?"

Does It Matter? is the title of a book of essays by the incomparable Alan Watts. The point of the book, in his words, is "to focus attention on what is happening as distinct from the ways in which it is described by words, numbers and other symbols." Indeed, that is the point of Korzybski's Razor as well.

So, put the question to me: "Is there free will or is the world determined?"

I would say: "Free will and determinism are words invented by humans. There are no such things in the world out there. They are ideas. You might as well argue over what color is better, blue or red? What does it matter? I take things as they come. And I don't think about 'free will' or 'determinism.' I don't see any advantage in settling this uninvited question. It really doesn't matter. To me, everything just happens. It's all one movement. Everything is connected to everything else. And so everything is the way it is because everything else is the way it is."

Some may find this answer off-putting. Most people I talk to about my ideas around the Razor don't like it. They feel hemmed in somehow, as if I'm telling them what they can and can't think about. I am not saying that. You can entertain thoughts about whatever you like. To me, Korzybski's Razor is freeing. It means you should *not* feel hemmed in by words (or abstractions generally). It means there are no Yezidi circles for you. Free will? Determinism? They are words first of all. Ideas. With that in mind, your creativity ought to be unleashed, not shackled. I gave you my response to the question on free will and determinism, using the Razor. But you can craft a different answer with the same tool, maybe better.

Further, let us not lose sight of the polar nature of these ideas. Logically, we cannot have one without the other. They are connected. To say everything is determined is to ignore the polarity of the concept. You must have agency, or free will, as an idea as well. Or else the concept of determinism makes no sense at all in the same way you cannot say everything is 'up'—because the 'up' requires 'down' to even be recognized. (And yet, as pointed out earlier, we have a certain paradox with 'free will' and 'determinism' seeming unable to coexist in the world out there).

Polarities are hard masters. They allow no nonsense. The very idea of determinism requires its opposite. Free will requires its opposite. You cannot escape it. To admit the presence of one is to admit the present of the other. The only way out of this paradox is to surpass the idea of both.

Accepting What We Cannot Comprehend

I mentioned Alan Watts. The discussion above reminds me of a line from his *Wisdom of Insecurity*: "Part of man's frustration is that he has become accustomed to expect language and thought to offer explanations which they cannot give."

To try to solve all the world's mysteries with language and thought is, in a sense, to try to make the world something other than what it appears to be. It is to prefer a painting of the Grand Canyon to the real thing, or to prefer a photograph of an ambling brook in a shaded wood to actually being there. These are abstractions of a moment, and yet the world out there is ever changing and complex.

Likewise, to fix certain ideas or definitions 'permanently' (even the idea of permanence itself) is, to use Watts's phrase, "like having fallen desperately in love with an inch." Our abstractions are like inches and miles, like degrees celsius or kilograms. You can know how tall a person is and how much they weigh at a given point in space-time, but you can never capture the complexity of that person in the fullness of their evolving life.

It is not only our ability to separate our abstractions from the world out there; we also mistake memories for actual events. As Watts points out, our memories of past events are actually part of our current experience. There is no separate self observing all of these things as if they were articles of clothing you put on and take off. They are indelibly melded together. There is only the present. To put it another way, there is no separate 'experience' and 'experiencer.' They are one.

This folds into our discussion of the illusion of a separate "I." Everyone is an expression of everything else. You are an expression, or the result, of the entire universe and everything that has ever happened. "The universe 'peoples,'" as Watts puts it.

We're all part of one movement, as the old wizard told me: "In the world, what 'is' is one… All concepts, ideas, divisions are imposed by the mind. They cover up 'what is' like a thick blanket of snow."

Speaking of the old wizard, it is time to come back to him one last time…

CHAPTER SEVEN

Hermes Trismegistus

Almost two years after my initial encounters with the wizard, I finally made a startling connection. It came out of nowhere, completely unforced. It just happened. I have to start with some history first, and then we'll visit one last time with the wise mage.

***

When I was a kid, I had daydreams of a wise old wizard. He wore a long flowing blue robe that ran all the way to his feet, covered in silver moons and yellow suns. He had a white beard, wore a pointed cap; holds an orb, like a giant marble, sometimes the size of a baseball, sometimes bigger. And so it is no surprise the image that came to me in my dreams—those interludes—was an old wizard...

As a pre-teen and teenager, I played a lot of *Dungeons & Dragons*. It was the 1980s and

the game was popular among my friends.
I created my own characters and my favorite was this wizard, just like the one in my dreams. This character was someone I would 'be.' And through him, I would go on many adventures. He became a familiar figure of my imagination.

I named him Marduke, inspired by Marduk—the chief god of the Babylonians. I had come across the name, possibly in a volume of my *Encyclopedia Britannica* (if you remember those!) or maybe in one of the books of mythology I owned, such as *Bulfinch's Mythology*. I spent hours flipping through these books. In any case, I just liked the name, which seemed appropriate for a wizard and added the "e" to ensure people would say it correctly to my ears.

As part of the game, I used to collect these lead figures, 2-3 inches tall, little game pieces that people used to represent different characters and monsters. There were a seemingly endless variety of them: knights, goblins, thieves, dwarves, elves—a menagerie of wondrous creations that you could play, or encounter, in the game. It was common to have such miniatures and paint them in creative ways. I did this as well.

Once, my best friend (who also loved D&D) and I got to go to a big mall in Atlanta—which was an hour away. This was a special treat, because they had a game store with many of those figures. As this was before the internet, going to this store was one of the few times I could even see any of these figures. And it was a magical experience.

I found a lead figure that very much resembled my wizard. He even held the orb, a tiny marble of glass. I painted his coat blue with silver moons and yellow suns. I painted his beard white.

Years later, as an adult, I would still sometimes have dreams or visions where this figure would appear to me. He was wise. And kind. And patient. A master of arcane knowledge. But I often forgot about him as I went about the busy world, immersing myself in other aspects of life, such as raising a family and in the acquisition of an education, wealth and a position in society.

It was only much later that the old man returned. Years and years later. And in a way I didn't even recognize at the time.

My wife and I moved in January 2022. One of the main attractions of the new house for me was the ground floor office, since I work from home (and have since 2004, way before it became a thing). Searching for a new picture to hang on the wall and that would have some meaning for me, I settled on an old etching of Hermes Trismegistus. He wears a robe and a pointed hat. He has a beard. Holds an orb. And beside him... are the sun and the moon!

For the whole first year this painting hung on my wall, I did not draw the connection to the wizard of my youthful days, hard as it is to believe now. (Just goes to show you how powerful the world's blinders can be, how they can so effectively silence and/or obscure that inner voice...)

Hermes Trismegistus

Then one morning I was sitting there looking at Hermes... and the connection dawned on me. And then I connected this Hermes with the old man in my visions I shared earlier. The realization was like a boom, like a whoosh, like a jolt of electricity. How had I missed it!

Now my interest in this figure greatly increased. I felt like the Universe was telling me something. This was a message of some kind, from the dead, from my deep self, from deep in my own subconscious, from... somewhere... I was meant to see this connection. I was meant to do something with it. But what specifically? I was not sure.

I had ideas. Was Hermes my prophet? The voice of my deeper self, like Jung's Philemon in *The Red Book*? Like Nietzsche's Zarathustra? My guide to that eternal wisdom? To the deepest knowledge of the self?

As I read more about Hermes Trismegistus, I had another powerful realization: Hermes is the mediator of opposites.

The Kybalion, which represents itself as a work of Hermetic philosophy (though it isn't really), speaks of the principle of polarity:

> Everything is dual; everything has poles; everything has its pair of opposites; like

and unlike are the same; opposites are identical in nature, but different in degree; extremes meet; all truths are but half-truths; all paradoxes may be reconciled.

Hermes, my Hermes, my wizard, teaches the overcoming of opposites or the union of opposites. It was a theme I kept coming across. I re-read Alan Watts' *Two Hands of God*, whose central idea is the unity of opposites. Watts opens with a quote from Chuang-Tzu, which, as we've seen, calls the apprehension of the good and bad, right and wrong as "the great principles of the universe" to which "all creation is subject."

He also includes a quote from second Isaiah, which shows the ancients of the 'Western word' knew full well of this principle: "I am the Lord and there is none else. I form the light and the darkness; I make peace and create evil. I, the Lord, do all these things." The author of these lines knew a god who was only good and only just was nonsensical—and also, I might add, too limiting. God would have to transcend such concepts altogether.

The ancient Greeks knew this as well. As the scholar Apostolos Athanassakis writes in his footnote on Artemis in *The Orphic Hymns*, "as with many Greek divinities, the ability to do one thing entails the capacity for its opposite." Artemis, for example, was a hunter of animals, but also protected them; she nurtured the young, yet also takes the blame for the premature death of children.

It is our lot as mortals to categorize and divide. It is our way of making sense of the world. We seem to always want to know what a thing is. We want to name it. As if naming it gives us some special understanding of what a thing *is*, or what we see or feel or taste or hear. We like names. We like labels.

And we seem to have lost our way, lost the thread of the great principle. As Watts writes in *The Two Hands of God*, "By and large, Western culture is a celebration of the illusion that good may exist without evil, light without darkness, and pleasure without pain."

One last point on this book by Watts—and I have a vivid memory of reading it in a grand old hotel in Stockholm overlooking Lake Mälaren—he mentions Hermes Trismegistus and his riddle of the Emerald Tablet:

> "Heaven above, heaven below;
> Stars above, stars below;
> All that is over, under shall show
> Happy who the riddle reads!"

The riddle points the way to self-realization, to enlightenment, to the goal of the grand project; the way is seeing opposites as merely human concepts, as our divisions upon a singular whole and then overcoming them.

This is what I would come to see as my path. Jung writes in *The Red Book* about how we all have to go our own way. He showed how he did it in *The Red Book*, using myths and images from the repository of the unconscious—a common bank of meaning embedded in images shared by humanity—and creating his own way. This book is an attempt at my own way, led and nudged this way and that by my own guide, Hermes, and populated by my own 'myths.'

Suddenly what enlightenment meant started to take on a special meaning for me—again to use the old analogy, a path opened; I could see where I needed to go. And Hermes led me to go deeper down this path. To keep with my own analogy, which he handed to me in earliest vision, the union of opposites led to the way out of the ruins.

Hanegraaff's Hermes

The best book I have ever read on Hermes Trismegistus is Wouter Hanegraaff's *Hermetic Spirituality and the Historical Imagination*.

Hanegraaff is the most respected scholar on Hermeticism working today. In this book, he digs in to find the authentic Hermetic tradition that stretches back to early civilization in Egypt.

Hanegraaff shows how this current of thought aims to transcend human concepts altogether and reach for a gnosis—a direct experience beyond words, beyond abstractions. This is a project compatible with my thoughts on Korzybski's Razor, the nature of polarities, and the unspeakable level. Hanegraaff's book shows Hermes Trismegistus to be a fitting saint, or patron, of that effort.

Hermes Trismegistus (or just Hermes for our purposes) is a legendary figure from the distant past, usually seen as a syncretism of the Egyptian god Thoth and the Greek god Hermes. He is a god or prophet, a master of ancient wisdom and magic. He was a great teacher and guide to spiritual liberation. His path was a joyful path, as Hanegraaff explores, that heals us of anxieties and fears. He aims to open us to the wonder of existence, to celebrate life and the light.

In Egypt, in the early centuries of the common era, people would gather in their homes to learn and practice this Hermetic path.

"But the Way of Hermes was not an easy path," Hanegraff writes. "It required patience and devotion, trust and discipline, diligent study, persistent practice, and a willingness to question conventional wisdom." It was a meditative path; there were no priests or ecclesiastical authorities, no books to memorize, no schools.

We have only fragments of what those teachings were and inklings of what those practices may have been. Hanegraaff's book is a wonderful piecing together of what we have. The main body of texts is collectively known as *The Hermetica*, or the *Corpus Hermeticum*.

The Way of Hermes emphasizes an experience that cannot be thought, it is not conceptual. It is not a philosophy, as Hanegraaff argues, but a spiritual practice. I find it hard to summarize, but Hanegraaff offers a quote from Michel Foucault on "technologies of the self" which seems fitting:

> [T]echnologies of the self... permit individuals to affect by their own means or with the help of others a certain number of operations on their own bodies and souls, thoughts, conduct, and way of being, so as to transform themselves in order to attain a

certain state of happiness, purity, wisdom, perfection, or immortality.

Hanegraaff says of this quote that it "is hard to think of a better short summary of what Hermetic spirituality is all about."

I can't get into all the aspects of Hermetic spirituality here, but I find parallels that seem to mesh well with things Korzybski and his fellow travelers would later write.

For example, in the *Asclepius*, a Hermetic dialogue in the *Corpus Hermeticum*, Hermes speaks of a divine source, or being, from whom we enjoy the gift of life. But he tells his followers that words such as "Father" or "Lord" are just for convenience. We use the words so we can speak and understand each other and try to carry on a dialogue.

But it is important to know these are just concepts, just words. As Hermes says, in a Korzybskian flourish, the spoken word is "a sound that is produced when our breath strikes the air." Korzybski too wrote of words as noises and "masturbation of the salivary glands." Korzybski and Hermes are brothers in their mindfulness of abstractions.

Hermes teaches we are slaves to "phantom images and illusions." Our concepts blind us to the underlying 'reality.' As Hanegraaff sums up in a striking passage:

> What the authors of the Hermetica are really telling us is that our faculty of imagination is being invaded on a daily basis by a barrage of information that severely constricts our consciousness—our inner world gets cluttered with meaningless junk or trash.

Our minds are so cluttered that we become fully enmeshed in the world of our concepts. We gotta have a certain job or salary. We need that trinket. Our team must win. We get angry over trifles. We embrace all the outward trappings of what society deems desirable. There is a restlessness and an unhappiness in this. And the Way of Hermes aims to cut through these images and illusions and liberate you.

What is this 'reality'? Again a repeated emphasis is that such things are unspeakable. Hanegraaff writes about the dialogue between Diotima and Socrates in Plato's *Symposium*. Diotima tells Socrates that neither she, nor can anyone else, can communicate 'reality' to him because it lies beyond words. It cannot be revealed that way, but only by way of experience. *Noesis* is the word used to express the idea.

Hanegraaff write how another Hermetic text, *The Ogdoad and the Ennead*, "culminates in a silent noetic (comm)union [*sic*] with the Source—a perception that is no perception, an experience that is no experience, and a vision that is no vision either, because there no subject to perceive or experience or see and no object to be perceived or experienced or seen."

I suppose such paradoxical language either speaks to you or frustrates you. Just let those words swirl around in your head. Try to get at what they are pointing towards. That is really what is going on here, a pointing—to noesis.

A Final Talk with Hermes

[One last conversation with Hermes, which comes in a hazy dream where we are in no particular place or time...]

Q: Where is civilization going? Is it doomed?

A: Civilization is in the nature of things and will resolve itself over time as it happens.

Q: Is everything that happens to us 'good' then, in that it unfolds according to some grand plan?

A: Everything that happens just happens. There is no 'good' or 'bad.'

Q: And is there a grand plan?

THE UNSPEAKABLE LEVEL

A: Plan requires a planner. There is no separateness. Both are the same.
Q: That is a cryptic response. I do not understand.
A: Think of the observer and the observed. They are of one movement, connected, integrated, not separate. So it is with the plan and planner.
Q: But who is the planner?
A: The planner is within; you are the planner.
Q: I do not feel like a planner. I feel like I am at the mercy of the plan.
A: That, too, is part of the plan. It is as you see it.
Q: You make it sound as if there is no God.
A: There is God as there are thoughts.
Q: God is only a thought?
A: There are thoughts as there are trees, mountains, and rivers.
Q: Those are physical things that we can touch.
A: Physical is another category of the mind, it implies also things that are not physical. See these categories are connected, as one and the same.
Q: But they are clearly not. I feel the sting of a bee.

A: Can you not also feel the sting of
a thought? They are the same.
Q: I struggle with you saying things are
the same when they do not appear
the same to me.
A: See them as manifestations of the
same thing. When you see a rainbow,
you can distinguish different colors,
but they are, still, all colors; in that
sense they are all the same.

CHAPTER EIGHT

Reflections: Beyond Polarities, Beyond Concepts

In the previous chapter Hermes points to noesis as beyond concepts. Here we reflect a bit more on the theme—as Julian, the former Roman Emperor, put it:

***

"Shall we write about the things
not to be spoken of?
Shall we divulge the things
not to be divulged?
Shall we pronounce the things
not to be pronounced?"

—Julian, *Hymn to the Mother of the Gods*

***

What if there is nothing other than the world as we experience it? Or is this, too, just another concept requiring an opposite?

THE UNSPEAKABLE LEVEL

Why do humans always—across all kinds of cultures and times—want to see the world as some kind of illusion, with a 'real world' behind it?

Is it because we can't stand the idea that this is it? That this ever-changing, chaotic, seemingly senseless world, and its cycles of birth and death can be the whole ballgame itself? That there must be some changeless, timeless something else beyond this?

I admit it is hard to accept. All that human wisdom, accumulated over centuries, is not something to dismiss lightly. We have testimonies, experiences, that point to something else—something at the edge of our consciousness—and beyond it.

Dreams, visions—true, they could all be powerful illusions... It is difficult to think through, but skepticism and doubt demand that you be skeptical and doubtful, too, of your skepticism and doubt...

Feeling and intuition tell me there is more than we readily perceive and grasp. It only needs to be unveiled. What is 'real' but another concept?

Hermes, the wise old wizard, speaks to me on this and his advice is clear: "Unify the opposites, transcend them and then see if these questions remain."

I have come to appreciate the power of looking at the world with the idea of opposites in mind. It helps navigate the claims of supposed seers and visionaries. If they do not confront the problem of opposites, then their claims never go beyond words.

To say, as certain new age approaches posit, that 'everything is divine' or that everything is sacred or that everything has consciousness, does not seem possible. These ideas run counter to the fundamental principle of the universe; divinity implies non-divinity; the sacred requires the profane; and consciousness requires its opposite, too. These dualities must be dealt with. Nothing is meaningful without its polar opposite.

We may disagree about what is opposite to what. For example, what is the opposite of 'love'? I would say 'hate,' but some might say 'indifference.' The exact opposite is less important than grasping that there is an opposite; that there must be an opposite; and that any concept forms a sort of polar field with its opposite—*and*, as polarities, they are connected.

So, God cannot be 'love.' Or rather, God cannot be *only* 'love.' God must also embody and embrace love's opposite. If not, then the opposite of love must exist elsewhere and then you have created a duality; there is God which is 'love' but there is also God's opposite (Satan, the old adversary, comes to mind). Then you must still unify these opposites; some early religious thinkers did just that and created yet another higher God that embodied these two.

(Sidenote: Why the monotheistic bias? Why not gods? I imagine I write to an audience steeped in monotheistic traditions. But monotheism, too, is a largely unexamined assumption. Perhaps all things are full of gods, as the Platonists say.)

Whatever course one takes to deal with such concepts, the opposites must always be recognized, seen as connected, essential, inescapable... and then overcome: unified, transcended and thus finally creating *nirdvandva*, freeing yourself from the power of opposites.

How to get there, wise old Hermes?

Hermes responds, "There is no 'there' to go to..."

Not This and Not That

What I am pointing towards is a non-concept that exceeds all concepts, the unspeakable level. Remember the quote from Rumi earlier in the book? "Out beyond ideas of wrongdoing and rightdoing There is a field. I'll meet you there." Where is there?

Let's try more pointing. Let us look at the Secret Book of John, one of the more widely known surviving texts of a gnostic sect called the Sethians and included in the Nag Hammadi Scripture. The Secret Book of John represents itself as revelation, given by the resurrected Christ, to the apostle John the son of Zebedee. It is a continuation of the fourth gospel.

But what is most interesting for our purposes is an early section where the text gives us a description of The One.

> The One is not corporeal
>   and it is not incorporeal.
> The One is not large
>   and it is not small.
> It is impossible to say
> How much is it?
> What [kind is it]?
> For no one can understand it.

In a footnote, the scholar Marvin Meyer writes that these statements are similar to the Hindu *Upanishad*, "with its insistence that the ultimate is neti neti, 'not this, not that.'" To me, it is a great example of grappling with opposites and trying to go beyond them.

But it is not the only example. Perhaps an even better, more evocative, text is the one known as Thunder, or Perfect Mind. Here are a couple of samples from the text to give you an idea:

> For I am the first and the last.
> I am the honored one and the scorned one.
> I am the whore and the holy one.
> I am the wife and the virgin.
> ...
> For I am knowledge and ignorance.
> I am shame and boldness.
> I am shameless; I am ashamed.
> I am strength and I am fear.
> I am war and peace.
> Give heed to me.

Again, the attempt to unify opposites, the pointing to something that lies beyond concepts.

Inspired by this, I once wrote out my own mini-version of Thunder in my diary:

> the giver of blows and the healer of wounds
> the order and the chaos
> the mistake and the correction
> here before the beginning and
>   here after the end
> old and young
> peaceful and violent
> the builder of all things and the
>   destroyer of all things

all these things and none of these things
free of all names, devoid of all images
nameless, formless

Can this make sense? Or is it a mere piling up of words? I feel there is wisdom here, but wisdom that is difficult to extricate, to pull from ore that lies deep in our consciousness under miles of the rock of accumulated conceptual layerings.

I find solace in contemporaries, wherever I find them, who are struggling with the same intuitions. Frater Acher, for example, in his book *Holy Heretics*.

Vices and Virtues

Frater Acher is a pen name, and I do not know much about the person behind the nom de plume. He is a contributor to an online book review site called Paralibrum where he is described as "a lone practitioner of the magical and mystical path." This "about" paragraph also includes a bit about his educational background (he has certifications in Gestalt Therapy) and notes that he "is a German national, and after several years of living abroad, he is now resident in Munich, Germany."

More importantly, he is the author of several fascinating books about what is sometimes called 'the western magical tradition.' I have read all of his books with interest and always learn something as he ranges widely over figures such as St. Cyprian of Antioch, Trithemius, Paracelsus, and many others.

In *Holy Heretics*, Acher tackles, among other things, certain Christian mystics. We will focus here on Hildegard of Bingen (1078–1179), the polymathic Benedictine abbess who received powerful visions she wrote about in a famous work called *Scivias*.

Acher, however, draws our attention instead to a lesser-known work titled *Liber Vitae Meritorum*, or *Book of the Rewards of Life*. Here she lays out thirty-five vices offset by thirty-five virtues. Among the pairings: greed and fair satisfaction, envy and love, anger and patience, truth and falsehood, disbelief and faith, injustice and justice. Each polarity is understood by contrast to its opposite.

As Acher writes: "Force and counterforce, impact and recoil, achievement and expenditure, Hassle and gain—one cannot be understood without the other... [The virtues'] radiant beauty is a direct function of the proximity of their nocturnal opposites." Each virtue shines only by the light given of its opposite vice; and vice versa.

Acher uses Hildegard of Bingen's teachings as a launching point to make the case that we need to understand the totality of these concepts, not to choose one or other, but to work with both, to see them as a whole. Like "a lock and key" the opposites "click into place."

Much like what I am pointing to in this book, Acher points to a way of thinking, or way of being, that somehow brings opposites together and then transcends them. He is worth quoting in full here:

> From this a new kind of art might emerge: a practice that this time will be neither black nor white, neither vicious nor virtuous, neither chthonic nor celestial. A practice that embraces opposites, without judgment or attachment, in order to measure, align and center the polar forces of creation so they come to stop pushing against and instead begin to rest upon each other. What is required by us humans, standing in the polarity of a hundred vicious vices and a hundred virtues' voices, is not the knee-jerk resolutions of the apparent tension, but the calm weaving of a pattern that will bind both of them into one.

Later he offers a meditative exercise to get you in that hard to define headspace that involves reciting the following:

> For I Am who is Neither
> Neither dark, neither light
> Neither false, neither true
> Neither dead, neither born
> Neither here, neither there
> Neither found, neither lost
> Nor neither is who I Am

Neti, neti—not this, not that. I was struck by Acher's attempt here because it so closely mirrors Thunder and my own mini-version of Thunder. Acher's attempts as well as my own to use language to point to this undefinable, hard-to-describe headspace add to a history of similar attempts that include Pseudo-Dionysius, Meister Eckhart, Carl Jung, Alan Watts, among others.

I mentioned earlier St. Cyprian of Antioch, a legendary figure of the 4th century, a 'pagan' magician who learned all the arcane arts. He emerges as a liminal figure, able to move between this world and the next. There is a poetic self-description, included among other texts in *Ancient Christian Magic* (Meyer and Smith's translation):

> I am Cyprian, the great magician, who
> was the friend of the Dragon of the Abyss.
> He called me his son, and I called him
> father... I ascended up to the Pleiades,
> and they glided under me like a ship.
> I learned the whispers of the stars; I took
> possession of the treasures of the winds.
> I mastered the whole of astronomy.

To be brief, Cyprian converted to Christianity after seeing how impotent his magic was against the simple Christian faith of a young woman named Justina; his sorcery defeated by the sign of the cross. The two become paired in legend. Cyprian eventually rose to the status of a bishop and Justina to that of an abbess. They were martyred together in the year 304 during a Christian purge under the Roman Emperor Diocletian.

But the basic legend of St. Cyprian is relevant here because he is a bridge between opposites: pagan and Christian, good and evil, the earthly realm and the spiritual world. Acher wrote a book exploring the legend of St. Cyprian, titled *Cyprian of Antioch: A Mage of Many Faces*. In particular he focuses on "the many polarities embodied by the myth of Cyprian of Antioch"–which is no surprise, as those of us sensitive to polarities and looking for fellow travelers are bound to come across many of the same figures.

In my library at home, I have a statue of St. Cyprian of Antioch, as (another) reminder of the problem of opposites, the inherent polarities of our conceptual frameworks.

Lest you think I have gone off the reservation here, I will point out that not only mystics and magicians and mythological figures, but also worldly and praised philosophers have tried to point to this nonspace beyond words and concepts as well, the unspeakable level. The one that comes most readily to mind is Martin Heidegger (1889–1976).

Heidegger's Hut

I love the ideas in Heidegger's *Being and Time*, which is the only book of his I have ever read (so far). It may seem an odd thing to say about a book that is notoriously hard to read. But I was fortunate to find an able guide to help me work through the book. I would highly recommend Simon Critchley's excellent series of podcasts titled *Apply-Degger*, where he goes through the book with you, section by section. Patiently working through *Being and Time* is rewarding, as it opens you to new ways of thinking about your own existence and place in the world, providing entirely different ways to talk about it, different from all the philosophy that came before it.

Ever since I read the book in 2022, I've noodled on various ideas in the book, off and on. They are sticky, though I don't pretend to understand everything. But what I want to do is merely mark him as a fellow traveler and at least give a tiny glimpse as to why he is important for our project.

One of things that makes Heidegger difficult lies in what he set out as his goal. He is trying to start over, in a sense, and build up a philosophy without the usual vocabulary of mind and body, objective and subjective and so on. And to do this he creates his own language, or rather twists the one he has.

That's why we have all these seemingly strange constructions in Heidegger such as being-in-the-world or present-at-hand or being-towards-death. Moreover, to read Heidegger is to take on a set of words used in unusual ways—all that talk about 'unconcealment' and 'clearing' and 'equipment'—at least, as the German words are traditionally translated.

Another thing that makes Heidegger difficult is he is trying to map out this terrain I have been struggling with as well, an attempt to get beyond our conceptual baggage and see the world anew.

Mark Wrathall sums this up very nicely in his book *How To Read Heidegger*: "Heidegger viewed his task as a philosopher as very similar to that of the poet, and he was willing to torture the German language to help us understand experiences and things that cannot really be captured in words and concepts."

This approach evokes shades of what we saw earlier from Richard Rorty: the idea of philosophers as poets. Read Heidegger, then, as a sort of poet trying to point at things that are difficult, or perhaps impossible, to capture in words.

But I would say a baseline understanding of Heidegger begins with the idea that there is no division between us and the world; we exist in unity. We are not free-floating subjects or minds apart from our bodies and the things of the world. They are unified. We are 'world.'

We find ourselves in a world full of stuff. I type this at a computer, at my desk, in my study, in a house, on a street, in a town, and so on and so on. There is a whole context of which I am a constitutive part of. I am not some thinking thing hovering over the world. I am in and of it. The world may be analytically distinct, but we experience it as a whole.

To understand Heidegger's view, we need to, as Critchley puts, "avoid conceptions of the subject, subjectivity, mind, consciousness, person—that whole language, the subject object split, Heidegger is trying to oppose this old view."

Heidegger is trying to get us out of our usual conceptual framework.

Dare I say, Korzybski's thought, at extremes where I am pushing it, winds up in a very similar place. In fact, some might say he, too, twisted the language to try to get it to say what cannot really be captured in words and concepts. I think here of those hyphenated words he favored, such as "organism-as-a-whole-in-an-environment."

Our use of abstractions has a way of setting up Yezidi circles and making us afraid to step over them. Korzybski and Heidegger (and Acher and the rest) are trying to get over those drawn circles on the ground. In a sense, it is easy to transcend, or see through abstractions, because they were never really there—just as that circle surrounding the Yezidi boy never really bound him.

There are some things, though, which do seem to bind us all. Death comes to mind. Another abstraction? What to make of death?

Memento Mori

Gurdjieff ends his *Beelzebub's Tales* with a short speech by Beelzebub himself. Here Beelzebub says that every human being "should constantly sense and be cognizant of the inevitably of his own death as well as the death of everyone upon whom his eyes or attention rests." Only in this way, Beelzebub says, will human beings lose their egoism, their self-importance and their "tendency to hate others," which is the chief cause of all troubles.

This remembering of one's own death, encapsulated in the phrase "memento mori" is an old idea, going back at least to antiquity. It's usually translated as "remember death" or "remember you must die." Some may think it a morbid idea, but I do not think so at all. In fact, I find myself more in agreement with Beelzebub than not.

In fact, inspired by Gurdjieff's (or Beelzebub's) recommendation, I bought a silver ring with the phrase engraved on it and a small skull set between the two words. It's not large or garish, but it serves its purpose as a reminder.

I can report such a reminder puts the travails of life in perspective. Irritated by a certain politician or public figure? Remember they will be dead some day. Yes, dead. And so will you. So what is the fuss about? Do you want to consume precious life minutes concerned about this walking corpse? I don't. The pomp and circumstance of life will seem all the more absurd.

On other hand, you will enjoy those sweeter moments of life all the more. Sometimes on a warm, sunny day, I'll just be on my deck and admire the natural beauty around me. The trees, the sky, the birds, the breeze... Or think of those people you especially enjoy being around. You will appreciate those moments because you know they will not last. I find myself soaking those moments more deeply, embedding them in my memory more so than otherwise. This doesn't happen all the time, but I find I can remember such moments in more exquisite detail than when I was less "aware" of death's shadow.

Will such exercises bring on a certain sadness? I find they can bring on a certain philosophical wistfulness, but I wouldn't say they make me sad. Meaning, these exercises reframe experiences; I see the temporality of all things, but I also appreciate how this must be so. The great polarity is one of life *and* death, after all.

I have a weird interest in what people say on their deathbed. Or what they supposedly said, because these things are often contested or unreliable. I want to believe people gain some clarity in their final moments about some aspect of life. And that these last utterances contain some great wisdom for us all. One of my all-time favorite "last words" are those uttered by the famous economist John Maynard Keynes: "I should have drank more champagne."

There is an old thread in philosophy that the goal of philosophy is to learn to die well. Think of Socrates: calm, even cheerful, before he was to drink the poison. Gurdjieff was another. His attending physician, William Welch, reports in his book *What Happened In Between*: "I have seen many men die. He died like a king." He died in command of faculties, with his wits about him, serene and accepting of his fate. That is to die well.

The philosopher David Hume (1711–1776) is another who seemed to achieve the feat.

James Boswell—yes, that Boswell—visited Hume on his deathbed and was surprised to find him "placid and even cheerful." Partly his surprise stemmed from Hume's reputation as an atheist. Surely the old non-believer would recant in his final hours? Instead, Hume was "talking of different matters with a tranquility of mind and a clearness of head which few men possess at any time."

I think of another of my favorite mystics, the great Swede Emmanuel Swedenborg (1688–1772). Swedenborg did not seem to think death was a big deal. He died at the age of 84, after a life full of adventure and accomplishments across many fields. At his deathbed, his maid, Elizabeth Reynolds reported, "He was pleased, as if he was going to have a holiday, to go on some merry-making." Swedenborg believed death was just like slipping on a new set of clothes.

To me, these men are heroes. They have accomplished something great in their final hours. They each loved life. There is no denying any of these partook of life's pleasures. It is not as if they were eager to die. But they did not cling desperately to life or shed tears that their allotted time had come to an end. They had reached a certain contentment.

I think, too, of Bhagavan, who spoke of death in his *Talks*. He relates death to sleep. Do we fear sleep? We don't. "On the contrary," Bhagavan says, "sleep is courted and on waking up everyman says that he slept happily. One prepares the bed for sound sleep. Sleep is temporary death. Death is longer sleep." Death is when we go back to the state we were in before we woke up.

A contemporary thinker who used the idea of memento mori is Steve Jobs, the founder of Apple. In an address to Stanford's 2005 graduating class, he said:

> Remembering that I'll be dead soon is the most important tool I've ever encountered to help me make the big choices in life. Because almost everything—all external expectations, all pride, all fear of embarrassment or failure—these things just fall away in the face of death, leaving only what is truly important. Remembering that you are going to die is the best way I know to avoid the trap of thinking you have something to lose. You are already naked. There is no reason not to follow your heart.

That is the beauty and magic of memento mori. There is no sadness in any of this; instead there is life-enhancing freedom. My memento mori ring, in that sense, is a real ring of power, a talisman that gathers my attention and reminds me of a certain perspective in all things.

An Aside on Attention

That word 'attention' is worth spending some time on.

Most people do not give much consideration to what they allow to absorb their attention. Here I am going to recommend you think about attention in the same way you think about your diet. You wouldn't just willy-nilly put anything in your mouth. So, too, you should not give your attention to just anything.

The old adage says you are what you eat. In the same way, you are what you pay attention to. What else could you be? So, be picky about what you pay attention to. If you pay attention to toxic social media posts and wallow in conspiracy theories and nutjob politics, then that is what you are. In a very real sense, you have become those things. They are part of you. By contrast, what if you focus that attention instead on beautiful things made by hand, the wonders of the natural world and sublime works of philosophy? You would be different. Entirely so.

We need to flesh out this idea of attention. What are we talking about? What is it? By now, you should have a ready answer. It is, first of all, a human concept. It's an idea. That will prevent us from making an idol of it or feeling bound to somebody else's definition. The second thing we can say is that it has an opposite, which we could call inattention.

Attention is probably best described in action rather than defined per se. We know when we have it. We know when we don't. We have it when we are playing Jenga and trying to remove a block without knocking over the whole tower. We have it when we are circling over that five-foot putt with a bet riding on the outcome. (As Lee Trevino pointed out, nothing focuses your attention like having to make a putt for five dollars with two in your pocket.) We have it when we are writing, focused on trying to get those stubborn ephemeral ideas on a page, clothed in words. They never seem to come out exactly right, but I keep trying.

Attention plays an important role in Gurdjieff's teachings; in a way, nearly all of his practices are ways of gathering and focusing one's attention. Gurdjieffian exercises often make you aware that you are mostly not in control of your attention. Most people, most of the time, behave mechanically, Gurdjieff thought. We use the barest amount of attention needed to get by or to do the task we're doing.

I think this is true, and it's not necessarily a bad thing. When we walk, we walk naturally, we don't think a lot about it. We don't focus so much on every step, except in circumstances where it may be wise to do so, like when it is icy outside or when you are walking a narrow ledge in the Andes—as I have done—where a misstep could be a very bad thing. If I have to run to the grocery store, much of that action will require very little attention. And when I bring home the wrong item, my wife will say she wished I was paying more attention!

Inattention strikes just as certainly. I burn the vegetables because I am not paying enough attention. Or I trip or bang my head or drop food on my chest or I miss my turn driving. All times when inattention happens and the consequences bring us sharply back into attention.

Also, as Korzybski warned, we need to be careful about either/or constructions. So, not attention or inattention necessarily, but gradations of attention spanning a spectrum.

Gurdjieff would have you focus on certain things at times, just to get the feeling of what it was like to really have full command over your attention. When you eat, try focusing on every bite. Really chew and taste. See if you can keep it up for the whole meal. It is not so easy, which is telling. Attention is slippery; it seems to come and go, fade in and out. And we have only so much of it.

One of Gurdjieff' students, Christopher Fremantle, wrote a book titled *On Attention*. Fremantle makes the following wise observation: "It seems impossible to find a point where attention can be separated from life itself." And so I have found in writing about attention and trying to nail down 'what it is.' Because 'it' seems like all one thing; inseparable from life.

Further, he credits Gurdjieff with bringing "back into currency the idea that attention is the most powerful creative force in man." Which is quite a statement. But if you think about it, how many great things have come about when human minds put their attention toward solving a problem or creating a work of art? Attention is powerful indeed. So take care what you allow to grab yours.

CHAPTER NINE

Mutus Liber—By Way Of A Conclusion

"The wordless book, in which nevertheless the whole of Hermetic Philosophy is set forth in hieroglyphic figures, sacred to God the merciful, thrice best and greatest, and dedicated to the sons of the art only, the name of the author being Altus."

—*Mutus Liber*, first plate
[translation by Adam McLean]

"When you don't name things anymore, you start seeing them."

—Alan Watts, "Lecture on Zen"
[transcribed by Alan Seaver]

***

There was a mysterious book published in 1677 titled *Mutus Liber*, also known as the Mute Book or Silent Book. It is a book with no text, only images. There are fifteen plates—the final plate I have included here.

Mutus Liber is an alchemical work. According to Adam McLean—a man who seems to have dedicated his life to the study of alchemy—authors in the 15th century through the late 18th century published about four thousand alchemical books. It is a vast subject. (And I cannot recommend McLean's Alchemy Website highly enough for anyone interested in exploring this topic: www.alchemywebsite.com)

Nonetheless, even knowing nothing of the art of alchemy, you can appreciate the rich symbolism by gazing at that final plate. Look at the images that compose the plate.

There is the sun. There are two angels who appear to be raising up a man and crowning him, perhaps with laurels. There are two other figures holding up two ends of a rope. There are, ironically, the latin words (the only words in the book outside of those on the first and fourteenth plate): "Oculus Abis" means literally "eye abyss." As noted by the Angela King Gallery, "Oculus Abis... is translated by Eugène

Canseliet (Fulcanelli's editor) as 'thou departest seeing.' Which perhaps implies the risen man has achieved a kind of enlightenment and now leaves the earthly realm with the wisdom of seeing things as they are." There is also the fallen man, the sun and moon nearby. A ladder lies on the ground behind...

There is a lot to take in here. All those symbols have meanings. As McLean tells us, "Alchemy developed an amazing language of emblematic symbolism which it used to explore the world. It had a strong philosophical basis, and many alchemists incorporated religious metaphor and spiritual matters into their alchemical ideas."

We briefly skirted around alchemy back in Chapter 3 on Polarities. The idea of polarities and the union of opposites was a central idea for alchemy. As Jung points out, the alchemical idea of a *hieros gamos*, or chemical wedding, is one where the male and female are fused or melted into one. Alchemical art has many ways of depicting this union of opposites. For some examples, I will be relying on McLean's Study Course on Alchemical Symbolism.

Perhaps the most famous example is the sun and moon, which dot many an alchemical landscape. Another oft-used image is the male and female, often appearing as a king and a queen. Sometimes they can appear together in the same image, as the nearby woodcut from the Rosarium Philosophorum shows.

Other pairs can involve elements, such as fire and water, or even directions, such as two fish with one facing left and the other right.

McLean provides other examples of oft-used pairings; red rose and white rose, red and white, black and white, left-hand and right-hand, Mars and Venus, Saturn and Jupiter, head and tail, orb and sceptre, birds flying up to heaven and birds flying down to heaven. This is just a small sample of potential opposites. But it gives you a feel for how creative the alchemists could get and shows, too, how some

Rosarium Philosophorum, 1550

examples are not so obviously opposites.

Alchemists used these pairings in a variety of ways to show the coming together of opposites. Using male and female, for example, the alchemist could show a wedding scene, an hermaphrodite or a man and woman embracing each other.

One of my favorite examples of the merging of opposites is the ouroboros. This is the image of the snake (or serpent or dragon) eating its own tail—combing the opposites of head and tail. The nearby image shows one early depiction of the ouroboros from a 10th century manuscript.

The words in the center translate as "all is one." The ouroboros can express the unity of all things, their connectedness as

An ouroboros, circa 10th century

we've discussed. It can also represent the never-ending cycle of life and death. I have the image of an ouroboros on my wall, as well as a bracelet, to remind me of these things.

The meanings of these images were not always stable and could vary from text to text, even with a text. This makes it a frustrating art to penetrate. And people can spend years, a lifetime, studying alchemical emblems and commentaries. I have a collection of alchemical books; I love the art. The books are beautiful to flip through and put me in a meditative mood.

However, I am far from an expert, and I don't purport to expound on what the *Mutus Liber* says. (I like leaving it as a mystery anyhow, for you to work out on your own, if you dare!) What fascinates me about alchemy is how the alchemists tried to encode so much information in these sorts of images. The alchemists let symbols and groups of symbols (called emblems) carry a lot of freight in their efforts to communicate complex ideas.

Throughout this book we've talked about the difficulty of conveying experience into words. The alchemists seem to have great appreciation for that challenge and seemed to prefer images over words. For example, in *The Hermetic Arcanum* by Jean D'Espagnet, published in 1623, the author writes "philosophers do express themselves more pithily in types and enigmatical figures (as by a mute kind of speech) than by words." He cites works by alchemists such as Nicholas Flamel and Michael Maier where the "mysteries are fully opened." He notes how the images, though created long ago, are "perfectly to be perceived by us." As if the images were better preservers of meaning than words.

Later, he expounds further: "As for the matter of their hidden stone, Philosophers have written diversely; so that very many disagreeing in Words, do nevertheless very well agree in the Thing... since the same thing may be expressed in many tongues, by diverse expression and by a different character."

Images, too, are still abstractions. They still face all the usual limitations—they are still the invention of human minds. But nonetheless, they can elicit feelings and intuitions that are more difficult to capture in words. Where words are distrustful, images may prove more effective. A picture is worth a thousand words, as the old saw has it.

There is also some value in not naming things, or trying to not name them so readily. I recall in Nietzsche's *Thus Spoke Zarathustra*, where he writes, "May your virtue be too exalted for the familiarity of names…" This idea of not naming your virtue—because then it becomes something common—is a powerful one. The alchemists make use of symbols to protect the unspeakable, in a sense. To say more than can be said in words, to leave it open and alive. The idea fits with Korzybski's general semantics, too: the idea of the unspeakable level, that words leave things out.

In the talk cited in the epigraph to this chapter, Alan Watts uses the metaphor of color to make a point: To say a leaf is green is to say nothing of what the leaf really looks like; real leaves are not 'green', but are many shades of colors, even the same leaf has complex coloring. Watts's point is that the world of color is infinite, and it is only when we stop trying to fix our conceptions on things that we really begin to see them. Images can help us here where words cannot.

As Nietzsche says, if you must speak of it, "speak and stammer." Speak of it indirectly, metaphorically, or, as the wise alchemists knew, symbolically.

The Art of the Tarot

Another interesting example of a silent book is a deck of tarot cards. As with alchemy, the creators of tarot decks embed the cards with a rich symbolism drawn from history, mythology, religion, and philosophy.

If you thought tarot was just a fortune telling gimmick, you may be surprised by its long history (and alternative uses). The earliest tarot decks in existence date to the early 1400s and originated in northern Italy. Scholars seem to agree they began as playing cards and later became tools for divination and spiritual practice, though I would also cite a pair of well-researched books that claim certain tarot decks began as much more than playing cards. (More on this in a bit.)

Moreover, the variety of tarot decks may surprise you as well. Tarot decks follow a broad structure of 78 cards; there are 22 trump cards and the other 56 cards are spread among four suits. Even here, there is room for variation among different styles. The Minchiate tarot deck has 97 cards; it includes 12 cards representing the Zodiac, among other additions. The Mitelli tarot deck, by contrast, has 62 cards. It cuts the 2 through 5 pips from the four suits.

There is also an accepted progression and placement of certain archetypes: the sun, the moon, the chariot, the fool, and so on. But even within this structure there is ample room for variation. For example, tarot decks typically include a Popess and Pope card. In Besançon tarot decks, however, these images are replaced by images of Juno and Jupiter. Older Italian decks have a character called a Juggler. Later decks, such as in the Rider-Waite-Smith deck, the Juggler becomes a Magician.

I won't assume you have a tarot deck handy. It may help to share an image and see how many-layered they can be. Let's look at the Magician, the first trump card in the popular Rider-Waite-Smith deck.

Already, given our brief look at alchemical images, you can pick up on some of the opposites embedded in the card: the red and the white robe of the magician, the red roses and white lilies, and finally the Magician pointing up and downwards. This latter positioning recalls the Emerald Tablet, a foundational text in Hermetic philosophy attributed to Hermes Trismegistus, which declares "as above, so below"—once again, the unity of all things.

The Magician's belt is an ouroboros. A lemniscate hovers over his head. On the table in front of him are a sword, cup, baton and pentacle—the four suits of the Rider-Waite-Smith tarot deck. Perhaps indicating his mastery over all them.

Rider-Waite-Smith tarot card, 1909

And this is just one card, in isolation. In combination with other cards, they can tell a story and the meanings multiply. There are books written about deciphering the meanings of all the tarot cards, and of the many variants and styles.

Today, the variety of tarot decks seems infinite, with new ones coming out every year, based on every conceivable theme—movies, books, historical events, different cultural motifs, or nothing more than the imaginations of the artists creating the decks.

I mentioned earlier that some tarot decks may have originated as more than just playing cards and mentioned a pair of books that argue otherwise. One is *The Game of Saturn* by Peter Mark Adams. He argues that the Sola Busca tarot deck, the oldest complete deck in existence, encodes "a set of philosophical, historical, literary and magical sources into a visual format."

The other is *The Tarot of Marsilio* by Christopher Poncet, who argues the widely popular Tarot de Marseille was created by the Renaissance philosopher and magus, Masilio Ficino. In his telling, the cards were part of an initiation and a way to pass knowledge and wisdom concealed from the uninitiated.

Clotho the Spinner from Carte Fine al Mondo c.1725-1770
(Marco Benedetti production, used with permission)

MUTUS LIBER—BY WAY OF A CONCLUSION AND A WAY FORWARD

Ever since I discovered the deeper symbolism of tarot, I've become an enthusiast and have collected over fifty decks, all historical decks from the 15th to 19th century. I don't use them for divination. But I enjoy looking at the cards and the mood they create when you pull a few and put them on a stand on your desk. They are meditative and facilitate creative thought. They help get you out of your usual conceptual headspace.

For example, take a look at the Sun card from the Carte Fine al Mondo, a Bolognese deck from c. 1725–1770, as reproduced by the talented cardmaker, Marco Benedetti. (Image reproduced with his kind permission.) The woman holding the distaff and spindle is likely Clotho, the youngest of the three fates. She spins the thread of life. Her sister Lachesis measures the length of the thread and Atropos cuts it, ending life.

Clotho is a creative force: she sets life in motion, she begins the process of birth and becoming. The sun, in Neoplatonic and Hermetic traditions, is often seen as a visible manifestation of the divine, a source of life and clarity. In tarot, the sun card is traditionally a sign of happiness, prosperity, good health, and success.

In combination, the two images create a wonderful synthesis. It speaks to me of the rhythm of life and the cycles of the sun. It brings to mind thoughts of destiny and how little is in our control. The warmth and light of the sun card seem a benevolent presence over Clotho as she spins her threads.

I could go one, but this gives you an idea of how such images can embed meaning. They also invite multiple interpretations. I know even looking at the same card on a different day brings different insights and moods and intuitions—which words struggle to convey.

Tarot, then, is another silent book, a way to get beyond words, to the unspeakable level. For that reason, specifically, I find it of great interest, along with alchemical symbolism.

There is another area I want to get to on this theme of silent books or experiences that are hard to convey in words...

The One

You may recall that Hermes Trismegistus told me he was the one who knows himself. I'd like to circle back on that idea, which takes us to a tradition deeply embedded in 'western culture' and where I would like to end our explorations: the Platonic tradition, which encompasses the philosophy of Plato and his chief expositors Plotinus, Porphyry, Iamblichus, Proclus, among others.

The Platonic philosophers were interested in how to live in the wisest possible way for your own enlightenment. As Tim Addey puts it in his book *The Seven Myths of the Soul*: "The philosophy championed by Plato is not the clever juggling of sophisticated crossword puzzles: *it is the yoga of enlightenment*" [italics in the original]. Philosophy is work on one's self, a devotional and spiritual practice. This is not the reading of Plato you got in school.

At the entrance of the sanctuary of Apollo at Delphi, the famous injunction "Know Thyself" greets visitors. Know thyself was (and is) the cornerstone of the Platonic tradition. To know yourself, though, you have to know more about your place in the cosmos. And that requires a lesson in Platonic metaphysics.

And perhaps the most central starting point here is the idea of the One, or the Source. It's hard to say what it is because it is ineffable and unnameable. You will find Platonic philosophers apologizing for even calling it the One, or trying to give it a name at all. (Perhaps the most forceful on this point is Damascius, the last head of the Platonic school of Athens, who died in the middle of the 6TH century.) Likewise I apologize for what is bound to be a clumsy description.

But we must try. The Source is, as the name implies, the source of all things and it is in all things, uniting everything. The world is one big connected thing, a unity.

Let us hear from Plotinus, who gives some good analogies:

> For if deprived of unity, they are no longer that which they were said to be. For neither would an army, or a choir, exist [as such], unless each of them was one. Nor would a herd exist, if it were not one. But neither would a house or a ship have an existence, unless they possess the one; since a house is one thing, and also a ship, which one if they lose, the house will no longer be a house, nor the ship a ship. (from Thomas Taylor's *Collected Writings of Plotinus*)

We are waves in an ocean, drops of water in a river, leaves from a tree. Different but not separate. All participate in the One, as Proclus wrote. The great Platonic thinker made this the first of his 211 propositions in his *Elements of Theology*.

The One is akin to the Tao, the way of the universe. And for Taoists, too, the Tao was an essential starting point for understanding:

> If you don't realize the source,
> you stumble in confusion and sorrow.
> When you realize where you come from,
> you naturally become tolerant,
> disinterested, amused,
> kind-hearted as a grandmother,
> dignified as a king.
> Immersed in the wonder of the Tao,
> you can deal with whatever life brings you,
> and when death comes, you are ready.
>
> –*Tao Te Ching*, 16

To try to sense the One, or the Tao, is to sense the ephemeral and transitory nature of our immediate and experiential 'world,' which we coat in conceptions and abstractions. These abstractions are our stories. As Sallust wrote, "The world may very properly be called a fable." And each of us has a part to play in the tale. Yet we should be mindful of how much weight we give these stories. We can tell different stories.

The Platonic thinkers did not reject the images and abstractions we form about the world. Rather, they sought to remind us that these representations —though often useful or even necessary —do not possess the ultimate reality we sometimes ascribe to them. The problem lies not in the act of abstraction itself, but in mistaking these derived forms for the realities they only partially reflect. Our metaphor, throughout this book, for elevating abstractions to this level has been the Yezidi boy and his circle. But as I hope is clear by now, we do it ourselves with any number of abstractions—our identities, for example, be they religious, ethnic, professional, social, or whatever.

The One, in its ineffability, is akin to Korzyski's unspeakable level. Korzybski comes close to the mystical One and the Tao in the pages of his *Science and Sanity*:

> The objective level [the world out there] is *not* words, can *not* be reached by words alone, and has nothing to do with 'good' or 'bad'; neither can it be understood as 'non-expressible' by words or 'not to be described by words,' because the terms 'expressible' or 'described' already presuppose words and symbols.

Both the Platonists and Korzybski see the interconnectedness of all things. The unspeakable level is part of everything. But we must make sense of this unspeakable world. For Korzybski the emphasis is on structure. We see a blade of grass as something distinguishable from what is around it, but we ought to also see it as part of a complex web of relations, an ever-changing process with a structure.

Platonists, too, parse reality in a similar manner with attention to structure. As Socrates says in *Phaedrus*, things "should be cut into species according to members, naturally; not by breaking any member, like an unskilful cook." I imagine a chef running his knife effortlessly along the joints. We should take care how we make our cuts, so to speak, in how we divide the world out there.

Ultimately, we realize that we can only really reach that unspeakable level in silence. "Here we come to one of the most difficult steps in the whole training," Korzybski writes. "This 'silence on the objective level' involves checking upon neutral grounds a great many 'emotions,' preconceived ideas,' etc."

So we are back to a deep, meditative silence as we try to take in the world in all its great splendor and connectedness without carelessly breaking it into conceptual pieces. I'm reminded of the words of Gandalf in Tolkien's *Lord of the Rings*: "He that breaks a thing to find out what it is has left the path of wisdom."

Is that not the source of so much trouble in the world? We break things apart without regard to how they are parts of the whole. Instead let's learn to see the whole and not lose track of it.

Coda

All of these ideas we have covered in this book are ways of seeing. Or perhaps even better, they are ways of revealing.

Revealing what? They are ways of revealing the world we veil in our abstractions.

What is that world like? It is a world of greater wonder and mystery and beauty than we suppose. It is astonishing in its complexity and unbelievably vast in its scope. It is ever-changing and connected.

We participate in it. We *are* it. And it is us.

All the sages we have consulted aim to take us to this unveiled place, this ineffable haven of authenticity and genuine experience.

Once here, we live with great humility and thoughtfulness and with appreciation for the mystery and depth of that unspeakable level.

Yes, use those abstractions. They are what we draw from the world and they are incredibly helpful in everything we do. They make Korzybski's precious time-binding possible. But retrace your steps also; don't forget the source, the unspeakable level.

BIBLIOGRAPHY

Acher, Frater. *Cyprian of Antioch: A Mage of Many Faces.* Quareia Publishing, 2017.

Acher, Frater. *Holy Heretics.* Scarlet Imprint, 2022.

Adams, Peter Mark. *The Game of Saturn.* Scarlet Imprint, 2017.

Addey, Tim. *The Seven Myths of the Soul.* Prometheus Trust, 2000.

Angela King Gallery. https://www.angelakinggallery.com/new-page, accessed July 7, 2025.

Aristotle. *Metaphysics.* Princeton University Press, 1995

Ashtavakra Gita. Shambhala Publications, 1990.

Athanassakis, Apostolos. *The Orphic Hymns.* Johns Hopkins University Press, 2013.

Baggini, Julian. *The Great Guide: What David Hume Can Teach Us About Being Human and Living Well.* Princeton University Press, 2021.

Barnstone, Willis, and Marvin Meyer. *The Gnostic Bible: Gnostic Texts of Mystical Wisdom From the Ancient and Medieval Worlds—Pagan, Jewish, Christian, Mandaean, Islamic and Cathar.* Shambhala, 2003.

Beer, Stafford. *Think Before You Think.* Wavestone Press, 2009.

Bhagavan. *Talks.* Sri Ramanasramam, 2016

Brunton, Paul. *A Search in Secret India.* Ebury Digital, 2016.

Challenger, Anna. *Philosophy and Art in Gurdjieff's Beelzebub: A Modern Sufi Odyssey.* Brill, 2002.

Columbus, Peter J., and Donadrian L. Rice, eds. *Alan Watts–in the Academy*, SUNY Press, 2017.

Copenhaver, Brian. *Hermetica: The Greek Corpus Hermeticum and the Latin Asclepius in a new English translation, with notes and introduction.* Cambridge University Press, 2000.

Critchley, Simon. *Apply-Degger,* https://www.onassis.org/channel/apply-degger-podcast-simon-critchley.

Curzan, Anne. "'Ain't' Is a Perfectly Good Word, Irregardless of What You Think," *Wall Street Journal*, March 16, 2024.

Cyprian of Antioch, St. *Ancient Christian Magic.* Trans. Marvin W. Meyer and Richard Smith. HarperSanFrancisco, 1994.

Dawson, William J. *The Quest of the Simple Life.* Bibliolife, 2007.

D'Espagnet, Jean. *The Hermetic Arcanum.* Aula Lucis, 2023.

Eckhart, Meister. *The Complete Mystical Sermons of Meister Eckhart.* The Crossroad Publishing Company, 2009.

Foucault, Michel. *Technologies of the Self.* University of Massachusetts Press, 1988.

Fremantle, Christopher. *On Attention.* Indications Press, 1993.

Godman, David. *Be As You Are: The Teachings of Sri Ramana.* Arkana: 1985.

Gurdjieff, Georges Ivanovitch. *All and Everything: An Objectively Impartial Criticism of the Life of Man or Beelzebub's Tales to His Grandson.* Dutton, 1964.

Gurdjieff, Georges Ivanovitch. *Meetings with Remarkable Men*. Penguin Compass, 2002.

Hanegraaff, Wouter. *Hermetic Spirituality and the Historical Imagination*. Cambridge University Press, 2022.

Heidegger, Martin. *Martin Heidegger: Basic Writings,* edited by David Farrell Krell. HarperPerennial, 1993.

Hildegard of Bingen. *Liber Vitae Meritorum*, or *Book of the Rewards of Life*. Oxford University Press, 1997.

Hildegard of Bingen. *Scivias*. Paulist Press, 1990.

James, William. *Writings, 1902-1910*. Library of America, 1987.

Jobs, Steve. Commencement Address. Stanford University, 2005.

Jung, Carl. *Mysterium Coniunctionis. Collected Works, Vol. 14*. Princeton University Press, 1989.

Jung, Carl. *Psychological Types. Collected Works, Vol. 6*. Princeton University Press, 1990.

Jung, Carl. *The Red Book*. W.W. Norton, 2009.

Kingsley, Peter. *Catafalque: Carl Jung and the End of Humanity*. Catafalque Press, 2018.

Korzybski, Alfred. *Collected Writings 1920-1950*, Institute of General Semantics, 1990.

Korzybski, Alfred. *General Semantics Seminar 1937: Transcriptions of Notes from Lectures in General Semantics Given at Olivet College* Institute of General Semantics, 2002.

Korzybski, Alfred. *Manhood of Humanity* 1921. Institute of General Semantics, 1993.

Korzybski, Alfred. *Science and Sanity*. Institute of General Semantics, 2000.

Lao Ze. *Tao Te Ching: A New English Version*. Trans. Stephen Mitchell. Harper & Row, 1988.

Lewis, Cecil. *A Wish to Be: A Voyage of Discovery*. Element, 1994.

McLean, Adam. *A Commentary on the Mutus Liber*. Phanes, 1991.

McLean, Adam. "The Alchemy Website," https://www.alchemywebsite.com/

McLuhan, Marshall. *Understanding Media*. Gingko Press, 2017.

Maharaj, Nisargadatta. *I Am That*. Trans. Maurice Frydman. Acorn, 1973.

Mayer, Chris. *Dear Fellow Time-Binder: Letters on General Semantics*. Institute of General Semantics, 2022.

Meyer, Marvin. *The Nag Hammadi Scriptures*. Easton Press, 2007.

Nietzsche, Friedrich. *Thus Spoke Zarathustra*. The Modern Library, 1995.

Plato. *Plato: The Complete Works*. Hackett Publishing Company, 1997.

Plotinus. *Collected Writings of Plotinus*. Ed. Thomas Taylor. Prometheus Trust, 2000.

Poncet, Christopher, *Tarot of Marsilio*. Scarlett, 2025.

Postman, Neil. *Amusing Ourselves to Death*. Penguin Books, 2005.

Postman, Neil, with Steve Powers. *How to Watch TV News*. Penguin Publishing Group, 2008.

Proclus. *Elements of Theology*. Prometheus Trust, 2019.

Rorty, Richard. *Contingency, Irony and Solidarity*. Cambridge University Press, 2009.

Rorty, Richard. *Philosophy as Poetry*. University of Virginia Press, 2016.

Rorty, Richard. *Pragmatism as Anti-Authoritarianism*. Harvard University Press, 2021.

Roubineau, Jean-Manuel. *The Dangerous Life and Ideas of Diogenes the Cynic*. Oxford University Press, 2023.

Sallust (Gaius Sallustius Crispus), as quoted in: Taylor, Thomas. *Collected Writings on the Gods and the World*. Prometheus Trust, 2006.

Shamdasani, Sonu, and James Hillman. *Lament of the Dead*. W.W. Norton, 2013.

Smith, Cyprian. *The Way of Paradox: Spiritual Life as Taught by Meister Eckhart*. Paulist Press, 1987.

Suzuki, D. T. *The Selected Works of D.T. Suzuki,* Vol. III. University of California Press, 2016.

Taylor, Thomas. *Collected Writings of Plotinus*. Prometheus Trust, 2021.

Toksvig, Signe. *Emmanuel Swedenborg: Scientist and Mystic*. Swedenborg Foundation, 1983.

Tolkien, J.R.R. *Lord of the Rings*. William Morrow, 2015.

Walker, Kenneth. *A Study of Gurdjieff's Teaching 1957*. Jonathan Cape, 1957.

Watts, Alan. *Does It Matter?* New World Library, 2007.

Watts, Alan. *Psychotherapy East and West*. New World Library, 2017.

Watts, Alan. *The Two Hands of God.* New World Library, 2020.

Watts, Alan. *Wisdom of Insecurity.* Vintage Books, 2011.

Welch, William. *What Happened In Between: A Doctor's Story.* George Braziller, 1972

Wrathall, Mark. *How To Read Heidegger.* W.W. Norton, 2006.

A

abstractions, xii, 221–22, 224
  assumptions underlying, 1–3
  defining, xviii–xix
  definitions and, 160–61
  dismissal of, 110–11
  higher and lower order, 9
  images as, 210
  Korzybski and, 17–20, 33, 52, 59, 193
  meanings and, 1–3
  polarities and, 61–86
  as rainbow, 152
  ranking of, 10–11
  Rorty and, 138–39
  seeing through, 107
acceptance, 128–29, 160–62
Acher, Frater, 185–86, 193
Adams, Peter Mark, 215
Addey, Tim, 219
alchemy, 79–80, 205–11, 218
Angela King Gallery, 205–6
antithesis, 67–68
archetypes, 212–13
Aristotle, 52, 64
  essentialism of, 143
  Metaphysics, 97, 144
Artemis, 168–69

Asclepius, 173
ascriptionless existence, 113
The Ashtavakra Gita, 50, 53, 54-55, 118
assumptions, 1-2
Athanassakis, Apostolos, 168-69
attention, xxiii, 199-202
authenticity, 224

B
Béguines, 66
Benedetti, Marco, 217
Besançon tarot decks, 213
Bhagavan, 198.
 See also Maharshi, Ramana (Bhagavan)
books, 123-25
Boswell, James, 197
Brunton, Paul, 113
Buddha, 86
Buddhism, 65
Bulfinch's Mythology, 164
Burroughs, William, xxi

C
Canseliet, Eugène, 205-6
Carte Fine al Mondo, *216*, 217
causality, 104
certainty, 53
chain index, 88-89
Challenger, Anna, 30-32
Christian mystics, 79-80, 186
Christianity, 79-80, 186, 189

Chuang-Tzu, 62, 168
Clotho, *216*, 217, 218
coincidentia oppositorum, 66, 84
color, metaphor of, 211
compassion, 106–7
concepts, 131–33, 179
   blindness and, 173–74
   limitations of, 71
   polarities and, 62–63, 159
   seeing through, 77
   world beyond, 151–52
connectedness, 110, 130, 142–45, 182, 208–9, 222–23
Corpus Hermeticum, 172, 173
Cratylus, 97
cravings, 118
creativity, 141–42
Critchley, Simon, 190, 193
Curzan, Anne, 34–35
Cynics, 111–12
Cyprian of Antioch, St., 186, 188–90

D

Damascius, 219–20
Darwin, Charles, 52
Dawson, William J., 35–37
death, 194–99
definitions, xx–xxi, 160–61
   abstractions and, 160–61
   resistance to, 72

'democracy,' 8
descriptions, 10, 67, 107, 112, 139–41, 145, 146–47, 149, 222
D'Espagnet, Jean, 209–10
detachment (*gelassenheit*), 65, 68–69, 109
determinism, vs. free will, 154–60
Dewey, John, 138
dictionaries, 34–35
Dil, Answar, 21–23
Diocletian, 189
Diogenes, 111–12
Diotima, 174
Dorn, Gerhard, 79–80
doubt, 151, 180
dreams, 39–59, 180
dualism, 67
Dungeons & Dragons, 163–65

E

Eckhart, Meister, 64–66, 68–70, 74, 79, 188
ego, 77, 87–114. *See also* "I"; the self
Egypt, ancient, 171–72
Einstein, Albert, 21–23, 31, 52, 90–91
either/or constructions, 201–2
Eleusinian Mysteries, 114
Eliot, George, 2
emblems. *See* symbols/symbolism
Emerald Tablet, 213
Empedocles, xvii, 144
enlightenment, 84, 170

Epicureanism, 111
'equality,' 8
equanimity, 128–29
essentialism, 143, 144–45
ETC, 138
Euthyphro, 137
events, engine driving, 103–4
everything hypothesis, 104–5
evil, 84–85, 115
exile, 112
Exodus, 99
experience, 134, 137, 161, 175, 221
   speaking from, 110
    "unspeakable level" of, 97

F
failure, 23–25
fate, 155
feeling, 180
Ficino, Masilio, 215
Flamel, Nicholas, 210
"folk psychology," 153–54
forms, 221–22
Foucault, Michel, 172–73
the Fourth Way, xxii
free will, vs. determinism, 154–60
Fremantle, Christopher, 202
Frydman, Maurice, 101, 102
Fuller, Buckminster, xvi–xvii, xxi, 20–25

G

general semantics, xx–xxi, 4–5, 138–39, 142–43, 211
General Semantics Bulletin, 138
Genesis, 84
gnosis, 171
gnostics, 183
God
   as *coincidentia oppositorum*, 66
   surpassing descriptions, 67
Godman, David, 26–27
good, 83–84
Greeks, ancient, 112, 114
Gregory of Nyssa, St., 58
Gurdjieff, George, 20, 30–32, 47
   All and Everything: An Objectively Impartial Criticism of the Life of Man or Beelzebub's Tales to His Grandson, xxii
   attention and, xxiii, 200–201
   background of, xxii
   Beelzebub's Tales, 194
   the Fourth Way and, xxii
   Gurdjieffian exercises, 200–201
   Gurdjieffian metaphors, xvi
   Korzybski and, xx
   self-observation and, 94–95

H

Hanegraaff, Wouther, 170–77
happiness, 43
Heidegger, Martin, 65, 150, 190–94
   Being and Time, 190–91
   translation of, 191

Heinlein, Robert, xxi
Heraclitus, 95, 97
Hermes Trismegistus, 163–77, *166*, 179, 180, 182, 213, 218
The Hermetica, 172, 174
Hermeticism, 171–72, 217
Hicks, Bill, 11–12
hieros gamos, 206
Hildegard of Bingen, 186–87
   Liber Vitae Meritorum, 186
   Scivias, 186
Hillman, James, 153
holistic thinking, 95–96
housekeeping notes, xiii–xxx
human nature, 52
Hume, David, 196–97
humility, 76

I

"I," 87–114
   illusion of separate, 161
Iamblichus, 219
identity, 92, 97–98, 107–8, 221. *See also* the self
Ignatius of Loyola, 78
images, xviii, 1–2, 221
   as abstractions, 210
   alchemical, 203–11
   meanings and, 218
imagination, 39, 42, 48, 141–42, 146, 150
immortality, 109
inattention, 200, 201
ineffability, 70, 219–20, 222, 224

inferences, 10
Institute of General Semantics, xix, xxi, 88
interconnectedness, 222–23. *See also* connectedness
intuition, 180

J

James, William, 150–51
Jesus, 79, 84, 115, 153
Jobs, Steve, 198
John, son of Zebedee, the apostle, 183
journaling, 93
judgments, 133
Julian, 179
   Jung, Carl, xiv, 39, 65, 73–74, 78, 78–82, 79–80, 84, 129, 153, 188, 206
   active imagination and, 39
   coincidentia oppositorum and, 83
   hieros gamos and, 206
   The Laws of Manu, 73
   Mysterium Coniunctionis, 82
   Psychological Types, 73
   The Red Book, 78, 153, 167, 170
   Red Book, 153
   on religion, 153
'justice,' 8
Justina, 189

K

key concepts, xii
Keynes, John Maynard, 196
Kingsley, Peter, xiv, 152

Korzybski, Alfred, xix, 40, 52, 98, 108, 193, 222
  abstractions and, 138-39
  background of, xx-xxi
  chain index and, 88-89
  compared to Maharaj, 98, 101
  debt to, xxi
  on either/or constructions, 201-2
  general semantics and, xx-xxi, 4-5, 138-39, 211
  General Semantics Seminar 1937, 92-93
  Guitar Center, 108
  Gurdjieff and, xx
  Hermes Trismegistus and, 173
  Korzybski's plant and, 108
  Korzybski's Razor and, 1-37, 20, 40, 59, 61,
    85-86, 156, 157-59
  Maharaj and, 111
  Manhood of Humanity, 3
  "the map is not the territory," xii, xx, 19-20
  on not separating the inseparable, 96
  Olivet Lectures, 92-93
  resistance to definition and, 72
  Rorty and, 138, 142-43, 148-49
  Science and Sanity, xx, xxi, 4-5, 62, 89-92, 222
  structure and, 222-23
  three tools of, xvii-xviii
  time-binding and, 224
  "Time-Binding: The General Theory," 3
  unspeakable level and, xi-xii, 97, 138, 222, 223
Korzybskian extensional device, 143-44
Korzybski's Razor, xx, 1-37, 40, 59, 61, 84-85,
  149, 156, 157-59

The Kybalion, 167-68

L

labels, xi, xvi, 5, 20, 22, 23, 31-32, 107, 108, 113, 123, 143, 169
Lachesis, 217
language, 3, 134, 147, 193
   limitations of, 71
   words, xviii, 1-2, 222
The Laws of Manu, 73
Lewis, Cecil, xv, xvii-xviii
libraries, 123-25
love, 106-7

M

Maharaj, Nisargadatta, 97-99, *100*, 101-4,
   105-7, 110-11, 157
   on causality, 104
   childhood and youth of, 101-2
   everything hypothesis, 104-5
   I Am That: Talks with Sri Nisargadatta Maharaj,
     95-98
polarities and, 109
Maharshi, Ramana (Bhagavan), 26-30, 32, 39,
   57, 68-69
Mahāyāna Buddhism, 65
Maier, Michael, 210
Manu, 73-74
"the map is not the territory," xii, xx, 19-20, 140-41
maps, 17-19
Marcus, Robert S., 90-91

Maslow, Abraham, xxi
McLean, Adam, 205, 206, 207
McLuhan, Marshall, 15
meaning(s), 2, 33, 218. *See also* definitions
"memento mori," 194–99
metaphors, 206, 222
   of color, 211
   Gurdjieffian, xvi
Meyer, Marvin, 183
Minchiate tarot deck, 212
Mitelli tarot deck, 212
monotheism, 182
Moore, James, xxii
Mutus Liber (the Silent Book), xx, 203–11

N
Nag Hammadi Scripture, 183
names, 116, 169. *See also* labels
nature, 84
Neoplatonism, 217
'the news,' 11–16
Nicholas of Cusa, 66
Nietzsche, Friedrich, 150, 167, 210–11
nirdvandva, 72, 83, 182
noeisis, 174–75, 179–202

O
Ockham's Razor, 1, 19
The Ogdoad and the Ennead, 175
the One, idea of, 218–24
One Golden Thread, 99–100, *100*

opposites, 61–86. *See also* polarities
   freedom from, 72, 152
   Hermes Trismegistus as mediator of, 167
   as human concepts, 170, 179
   looking at the world with idea of opposites in mind, 181
   power of, 182
   St. Cyprian as bridge between, 189
   in tarot deck, 213
   union/unity of, 66, 79, 82–83, *82*, 117, 168, 180, 182, 184, 186–87, 206, 208–9
ouroboros, 208–9, *208*, 213

P

pandemic of 2020, 147–48
pantheism, 129, 182
Paracelsus, 186
paradox, 64–65, 67–68, 113, 175
Paralibrum, 185
Parmenides, xvii, 86, 152
paths, 154
Paul, St., 70
Pawley, Martin, 23–24
peace, 43
perceptions, 5–9, 10, 108, 175
Philemon Foundation, 78
philosophy, 114, 218–19
Plato, 218–19, 219
   Euthyphro, 137
   Phaedrus, 223
   Symposium, 174

Platonic tradition, 130, 182, 218–24, 219, 220–22
Plotinus, 219, 220
poetry, 141
polarities, 23, 61–86, 109, 159–60, 180–81, 186–87, 196, 206. *See also* opposites
principle of polarity, 167–68
Poncet, Christopher, 215
Pope, 66
Porphyry, 219
Postman, Neil, 13–15, 147
Powers, Steve, 14
Proclus, 219, 220
Przywara, Erich, 79, 84
Pseudo-Dionysius, 70–72, 188

R

the *Ramayana*, 73–74
reality, 146–48, 148–49, 156, 157
rebis, 82–83, *82*
Reid, Thomas, 9–10
relations, webs of, 142–45. *See also* connectedness
religion, 113, 151, 153, 182. *See also specific religions*
repetition, xiii–xiv
Reynolds, Elisabeth, 197
Rider-Waite-Smith tarot deck, 213, *214*
Rorty, Richard, 137–38, 139, 148–49, 154, 192
   affinity with general semantics, 138–39, 142–43
   Contingency, Irony, and Solidarity, 137–38, 150
   on essentialism, 144
   idea of philosophers as poets, 192

Martin Heidegger: Basic Writings, 150
Philosophy as Poetry, 141, 146–48, 150
Pragmatism as Anti-Authoritarianism, 143
Rosarium Philosophorum, 207, *207*
Roubineau, Jean-Manuel, 111

S

Sagan, Carl, xvi, 89
Sallust (Gaius Sallustius Crispus), 221
science, 147–48
screens, 127
Scult, Jeff, 99–100
Secret Book of John, 183
seeing, 133
the self, 87–114, 133–34
    'authentic,' 133–34
    authentic, 134
    ever-changing, 93–94
    as "fictitious entity," 90, 99
    "technologies of the self," 172–73
self-enlightenment, 84
self-identification, 97–98
self-observation, 94–95
self-realization, 170
Sethians, 183
Shamdasani, Sonu, 153, 153–54
Shaw, Bernard, xviii
signs, xviii, 1–2
silence, 223
skepticism, 151, 180

Smith, Cyprian, 66, 67–68, 68–69
Snyder, Robert, xvi–xvii
Socrates, 137, 174, 196, 223
Sola Busca tarot deck, 215
the Source, 220
Spinoza, Baruch, 52, 131
Stoicism, 111
Stoics, 69
Structural Differential (SD), xii, 4, *6*, 16
suffering, 43
Suzuki, D.T., 65
Swedenborg, Emmanuel, 197
symbols/symbolism, xviii, 1–2, 79, 203–11, 206, 208–9, 218, 222
synthesis, 218

T

Tao, 220–21, 222
Taoists, 220–21
tarot, 211, 215–18
Tarot de Marseille, 215
Taylor, Thomas, 220
"technologies of the self," 172–73
things, as numbers, 144
Thoth, 171
Thunder, or Perfect Mind, 183–85, 188
time-binding, 8, 52, 224
Tolkien, J.R.R., 223
Trevino, Lee, 200
Trithemius, Johannes, 186

truth, 145–46, 147–48
  search for, 137–38
  universal liability and, 150–54

U

uncertainty, 53–54
the unconscious, 170
unity, 66, 68–69, 220
  of opposites, 66, 79, 82–83, *82*, 117, 168, 180, 182, 184, 186–87, 206, 208–9
  with the world, 192–93
universal liability, 150–54
unnameability, 219–20
unspeakable level, 182–83, 218, 222, 223, 224. *See also* ineffability
  AI Gemini's explanation of, xi–xii
  of experience, 97
  Korzybski and, xi–xii, 97, 138, 222, 223
Upanishads, 183

V

via negativa, 119

W

Walker, Kenneth, 94
Watts, Alan, 23, 62, 65, 70, 77, 89, 161, 188, 211
  Does It Matter? 158
  Two Hands of God, 168, 169–70
  Wisdom of Insecurity, 160
Way of Hermes, 172, 174
Welch, William, 196

"western magical tradition," 186
words, xi, xviii, 1-2, 22, 23, 222
the world 'out there,' 136-61
Wrathall, Mark, 192

Y
Yezidis, xiii-xiv, xix, 222

Z
Zen Buddhism, 65

COLOPHON

....

This publication uses **Warbler**, a contemporary serif typeface created by David Jonathan Ross (DJR) and released in 2022. It captures the clarity and warmth of early book types while offering a versatile range for modern publishing. To distinguish the author's notes and inner directions to the reader, the sans serif **Frutiger**, designed by Adrian Frutiger in 1976, provides a clean, humanist counterpoint to Warbler.

For ornamental drop caps, **Goudy Initialen**, designed by Frederic W. Goudy in 1916, lends a decorative touch, echoing the tradition of illuminated manuscripts while harmonizing with the modern typography of this work.

These typefaces harmoniously blend historical significance with practical readability, embodying a sense of both tradition and contemporary style.

***

Choose poorly, and your type shall betray you...

ABOUT THE AUTHOR

Christopher W. Mayer is an independent scholar and author. His previous books include *How Do You Know?* and *Dear Fellow Time-Binder: Letters on General Semantics*, both published by the Institute of General Semantics. He enjoys homemade pizza, old philosophy books and trying to reach the unspeakable level.

www.ingramcontent.com/pod-product-compliance
Lightning Source LLC
Chambersburg PA
CBHW031620160426
43196CB00006B/216